Bush Foods

Nhenhe-areye anwerne-arle arlkweme

Arrernte foods from Central Australia

by Margaret-Mary Turner-Neale
with John Henderson

Arandic Languages Dictionaries Program,
Language Centre,
Institute for Aboriginal Development

illustrated by
Shawn Dobson

Arunta Art Gallery
& Book Shop
Todd Street, Alice Springs

IAD PRESS
Alice Springs

First published in 1994 as *Arrernte Foods: Foods from Central Australia* by IAD Press. This edition published in 1996 by IAD Press, Institute for Aboriginal Development, PO Box 2531, Alice Springs, NT 0871, Australia.
Reprinted in 1996.

National Library of Australia Catalogue-in-Publication data:

Turner, Margaret-Mary.
Bush foods: Arrernte foods from Central Australia = Nhenhe-areye anwerne-arle arlkweme.

ISBN 0 949659 90 8.

1. Wildlife as food – Australia, Central. 2. Wild plants, edible – Australia, Central. 3. Wild foods – Australia, Central. 4. Aborigines, Australian – Australia, Central – food. 5. Aranda (Australian people) – food. I. Dobson, Shawn. II. Henderson, John. III. Title.

641.300994291

Illustrations by Shawn Dobson, except where otherwise credited.
Design by Christine Bruderlin
Map by Brenda Thornley
Cover photography by Jenny Green
Printed by Robert Burton Printers, Sydney

Acknowledgements
Thanks to Veronica Dobson, Gavan Breen, Peter Latz, Jeannie Devitt and Jenny Green.

Publication of the first edition was financially assisted by the Arrernte and Warlpiri Curriculum Development Project administered by IAD.

Contents

PREFACE

The nhenhe mpwareme ingkerne-arle amangkemele aretyeke. Itne school itnekenhenge aremele akaltye-irretyenhenge, arrwekelenyele-arle atnyeneke-iperre-akerte. Arrantherre itele-aretyeke. Arrpenhemele-arlke aretyenhenge arrenhantherrenhe-arle akaltyele-anthemele.

Alhernterele apeke tyerrtye apmere arrpenhe-arenyele apeke aretyenhenge alakenhe-arle aneme-akerte akaltye-irretyeke.

I'm making this book for the ones who are growing up now to read, so that they will be able to look at it in school and learn about what the people before them had, so that you will all know these things. And so that your teachers can see this too.

I'm also doing this so that white people and people from other places can read this book and learn how things are.

Margaret-Mary Turner-Neale

INTRODUCTION

The Author

Margaret-Mary was born at Harts Range, to the north-east of Alice Springs, in 1938, and lived there until she was about eleven or twelve. She then spent a few years each at the Catholic mission at Arltunga and at Mt Riddock, before moving back to the Catholic mission which had by then been re-located to Santa Teresa (Ltyentye Apurte). She lived for a number of years in the girls' dormitory there under the charge of the nuns, before marrying in 1961. She has lived mostly in Alice Springs since the mid-seventies. She is very active in community work, and has worked over many years at the Institute for Aboriginal Development where she has taught Arrernte language to adults and has been a major contributor to the Arandic Languages Dictionaries Program.

The Language

There are quite a few different dialects of Arrernte and each one belongs to a particular area or family. These dialects make a kind of net where each is a bit different from its neighbours, and where, roughly speaking, the further apart their countries are the more different the dialects are. Most adults know a few dialects because people move around to different places to visit their relatives and often marry people from other areas.

Arrernte people identify themselves very strongly through their language, which is related to family, country and Dreamings. Even small differences between dialects are often felt to be very important, because they also distinguish families and countries. Arrernte people can identify their language at a range of levels, from a very narrow local or family dialect to larger regional dialects. Margaret-Mary describes the language of this book as Eastern Arrernte and it includes features of a number of dialects from this area. Her first language, from Harts Range, is described here, as in the *Eastern and Central Arrernte to English Dictionary*, as North-eastern.

The main communities where Eastern Arrernte dialects are spoken are Alcoota (Alkwerte), Harts Range (Artetyerre), Bonya (Uthipe Atherre), Santa Teresa (Ltyentye Apurte), Amoonguna, Alice Springs (Mparntwe) and out-stations to the north of Alice Springs.

There is a fairly large number of people who speak Eastern Arrernte, probably between 1,500 and 2,000, and it is fairly healthy, in that children are growing up speaking it. Arrernte language is used in many areas of everyday life, and in education and in the Aboriginal media.

In fact, the descriptions in this book were originally produced mainly for use in Arrernte

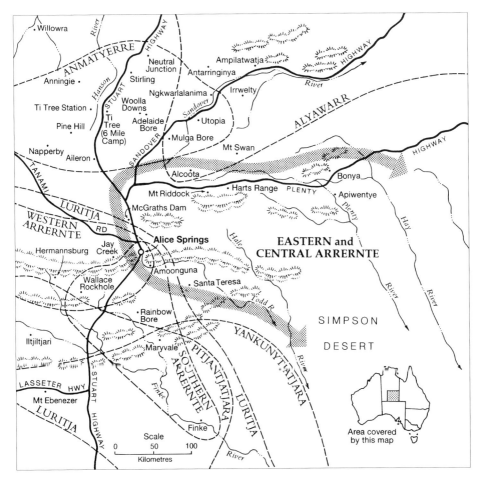

The Eastern and Central Arrernte region

Dialect areas in the Eastern and Central Arrernte region

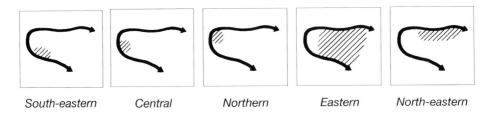

South-eastern   Central   Northern   Eastern   North-eastern

schools. The translations have been done with this in mind, and follow the Arrernte fairly closely, even if this makes the English seem a little cumbersome sometimes. The descriptions were originally recorded on tape, and although they were later edited after being transcribed, they still retain the flavour of oral language rather than a more formal written style.

Sounds and Spelling

The writing system used for Eastern Arrernte may look strange at first, but it reflects the way that the sounds of Arrernte work. Because of this, Arrernte people can acquire basic literacy skills in their own language fairly quickly. The sound system of Arrernte is quite different from other Central Australian languages or English, so we should not really expect its writing system to look like English or these other languages.

There are sounds in Arrernte which English does not have. For example, when the letter *h* is used on its own in Arrernte it represents a sound that is something like modern French 'r', or like an English 'w' but without the lips being rounded. This sound is not the same as English 'h'.

Another notable feature of the Arrernte sound and spelling systems is that pronunciation of the vowel that is written *e* is heavily influenced by surrounding sounds. For example, *e* after *w* may be pronounced as 'oo' as in cook, and *e* before *y* as 'ee' as in feet. When the surrounding sounds are ones which do not influence the *e* much, it is usually pronounced like the 'e' in father or pert, or even like 'u' in butt. As well, the final *e* written on all words is often left off in casual speech, as is the initial *a* in some words. The name of the language, Arrernte, is pronounced something like 'uh-RRUN-duh' (rhyming with 'under') or 'AH-rrun-duh'. The *rr* should be pronounced as a hard or rolled 'r' as in Scottish English. There is a guide to the pronunciation of the food names on page 68. See the introduction to *Eastern and Central Arrernte to English Dictionary* for more information.

Words and Grammar

Arrernte has a full and rich grammar, just as all languages do, but it is quite different from the grammar of English. For example, parts can be put into a verb to show how many people are doing the action, whether they are coming or going before or after the action, whether it is being done quickly, whether someone is doing the action to themselves or to others, and many other things.

This means that fairly complicated situations can often be described with a single verb, as in this example where someone is describing what will happen if two children continue to hang from a weak branch and it breaks off:

...re-atherre   arte+lh+artne-akerl+irre+tyenhe

he/she/it-two   cover-themself-quickly-go down-two doing this-future

The two of them will fall down and be covered (by the branch that falls)

This does not mean that Arrernte verbs are always this complicated, rather that they have the potential to be that way, a potential which allows enormous scope for creativity and verbal skill.

Endings on words are also used to express many of the things that are expressed by prepositions in English (to, for, from, at, etc.). For example, *kwatyeke* (kwatye = water, + ke = for) 'for water', *lhere-werne* (lhere = creek, + werne = towards) 'to the creek', *nhenhenge* (nhenhe = here, + nge = from) 'from here'. The common endings used in the story can be found in the accompanying glossary.

Food Categories

The foods in this book fall into the following categories:

kere	food from animals; meat, fat, offal, blood
merne	food from plants; fruit, vegetables, seeds
ntange	edible seeds
tyape	edible grubs and insects; witchetties, cicadas
ngkwarle	honey-like foods; nectar, wild honey, gum

These words can be used on their own to describe these categories or particular things which are included in a category, and they can also be used together with the name of a particular type or source of food. For example, *untyeyampe* 'corkwood flower nectar' can also be described as *ngkwarle untyeyampe* and *aherre* 'kangaroo' can be described as *kere aherre*.

There are four other category words used frequently in this book:

thipe	fleshy flying creatures; birds (but not emus), bats
kwatye	water in any form, sources of water; water, rain, clouds
arne	trees, shrubs, bushes, woody plants, some grasses
ure	fire, things to do with fire

Again, these words can be used together with the name of a particular thing that falls in the category, for example, *arne apere* 'red river gum tree'. Sometimes it is just the category word that distinguishes between something that is a source of certain food and the food itself, for example, *arne atwakeye* 'wild orange tree' and *merne atwakeye* 'wild orange (fruit)'.

Some things can be in two categories at once, and in these cases both category words can go before the name. Edible seeds are both *merne* and *ntange*, so pigweed seeds, for example, can be described as *merne ntange ulyawe*. Similarly, birds that are eaten are both *kere* and *thipe*, so ducks can be described as *kere thipe awengkere*.

Food and Cooking

Arrernte people today eat many non-traditional foods, and no longer rely on traditional foods for their survival. However, many traditional foods are still popular and are eaten fairly commonly. People living in Alice Springs and other communities often enjoy bush trips where they can gather these foods.

Not all the traditional foods that Arrernte people eat are described in this book, and some of the foods that are described here are not important foods and were not eaten very often by adults. Some, like small lizards, are mostly eaten by children, usually at the age when they get around in groups pretty much looking after themselves.

The descriptions of the foods in this book also include the methods that are used in cooking them. Many of these foods are cooked in *alpmanthe* or *arlpe*, the hot soil and ashes next to and under a fire.

Dreamings

There are Dreaming stories about most of these traditional animals, plants and other types of food, but these stories are not included here, because Margaret-Mary believes that it is more appropriate that these stories are told by the people who belong to each particular Dreaming.

John Henderson
December 1993

NGKWARLE
Honey-like foods

Ngkwarle is foods that are like honey, although some of them are not particularly sweet. It includes nectar from flowers, edible gum from certain trees, honeyants, and, of course, wild honey. It is also used to describe alcoholic drinks.

Ngkwarle athenge arlperle

Athenge arlpele apele nhenge
athengeke-arleke ineme. Akeme, arne
arntarlkweke ineme. Arrpenhe mape
athetheke anthurre, arrpenheme
akenhe arrerlkere, renhe ulkere inemele
nhenge athengeke-arleke. Arnenge-
ntyele thelelheme ahelhe-werne arlpentye
akngerre. Renhe akenhe ileme, 'Athenge
yanhe-ntyele athenge arlperle rlpmerre
tnyepetnyeme kwenhe.' Renhe imernte
inemele ulpe-ilemele kwatye akwekeke-
arle arrernemele, akernte-irretyeke
arrernemele. Arne intele imernte renhe
thankwemele arlkwemele, akernte aneme.

Ironwood tree gum

*You get the gum from ironwood trees.
You find it on the branches and you
break it off. Sometimes it's red
but other times it's clear when
you get the gum from the
ironwood. It runs down the tree
to the ground in long beads.
Someone might say it, 'The
ironwood gum is dripping down from
the tree!' Then they'd get it and mash it
up and mix in a bit of water and leave it to
set. You scoop it up with a little stick and
eat it when it's set.*

ARRERNTE: Ngkwarle athenge arlperle
ENGLISH: Ironwood tree gum
SCIENTIFIC: Acacia estrophiolata (tree)

2

Ngkwarle alkerampwe

Ngkwarle alkerampwe apele ineme nhenge artetyeke-arleke. Artetyele arle itne arntarlkwele anirtneme, arrerlkere mape anirtnerle, arrpenheme athetheke-arle. Nhenge apurte akweke mape-arle itne aneme. Nhenge arne inteke-arleke arrpenhemele inerle, arne intele atanthemele arneke-arleke. Iltyingke imernte ilemele, ikelhe ananerle-alpetyeke, arrernemele, anthemele ampele arlkwerretyeke.

Mulga tree gum

You get this gum from a mulga tree. You find bits of it sitting in a row on a branch of the mulga. There are clear bits and red bits. They are little round things. You get them off onto a little wooden skewer, skewering them straight off the tree. When you've got a bundle of these together, putting the bits on so that they sit all in a row, you can give them to the kids to eat.

ARRERNTE: Ngkwarle alkerampwe
ENGLISH: Mulga tree gum
SCIENTIFIC: Acacia aneura (tree)
A type of lerp scale is also found on mulga branches.

Ngkwarle arlperrampwe

Arlperrampwe renhe apele nhenge arne
ikwerele-arlenge anteye anerlenge,
arlperrele-arlenge. Ikelhe akngerre-
apenhe anerlenge, arrpenhe akenhe
anerlenge arlpentye ulkere arlpere-
arteke-anemele. Renhe apele inemele,
ikelhe-ilemele, urrknge-ilemele renhe
arrerneme. Ikelhe akngerre-apenhe
renhe mpwaremele, kele arlkwemele
aneme imernte renhe.

Whitewood tree gum

Arlperrampwe *is found on the trunk and
branches of the whitewood tree in big
globs. Some of it runs down the tree
trunk as if it's hanging there. You get it
and make it into a lump and knead it to
make it soft. You make it into a big lump
and then you eat it.*

ARRERNTE: Ngkwarle arlperrampwe
ENGLISH: Whitewood tree gum
SCIENTIFIC: Atalaya hemiglauca (tree)

Ngkwarle atnyerampwe

Atnyerampwe apele atnyereke-arleke
ineme. Nhenge arntapele-mpele apele
arrateme ware imernte ikiwemele,
arnele ayelpayernemele imernte
ikwerele inemele. Nhenge chewing
gum-arteke re-aneme
mwelpemwerneye. Unte imernte
arrkernemele anthemele, ampe apeke
anthemele. Kwatye anetye-akenhenge
arnterre arlkwerlenge akaperte
arntenhe-arntenhe.

Supplejack tree gum

*You get this type of gum from the
supplejack tree. You scrape it off when it
comes through the bark. You twist it onto
a stick to get it. It's a bit sticky like
chewing gum. Then you taste it and
maybe share it around, or give it to the
kids. If you eat too much without having
some water it gives you a headache.*

ARRERNTE: Ngkwarle atnyerampwe
ENGLISH: Supplejack tree gum
SCIENTIFIC: Ventilago viminalis (tree)

Ngkwarle akikarre

Atnyeme-arenye ngkwarle apele aremele ineme. Nhenge atnyeme antethe nhenge atnyerrirreme arraterlenge ikwerele-mpele akenhe ngkwarle rarle anirtnerlenge, arne atnartengele apeke. Athetheke arrpenheme, arrpenheme arrerlkere-arle. Renhe ikelhe-ilemele ineme, kwatye akweke arrernemele, arneke-arleke apeke ikelhe-ilemele arlkwerle.

Witchetty bush gum

You get this food from the witchetty bush. When the flowers start to fall, it comes out through the bark and forms in lumps, usually on the trunk of the tree. Some is red and some clear. You knead it into a lump sprinkling a bit of water on it. You can make into a lump on a little stick, like a lolly.

ARRERNTE: Ngkwarle akikarre
ENGLISH: Witchetty bush gum
SCIENTIFIC: Acacia aneura (tree)

Ngkwarle aperarnte

Wale aperarnte apele nhenge thelelheke-arle aneme, renhe imernte inemele nhenge apere irrkngelheke-arleke. Kele imernte nhenge ngkwarle re-akenhe anirtnerlenge irrkngelhe ikwerele-arlenge, arrpenheme akenhe nhenge ahelheke thelelheke ineme.

River red gum honeydew

Aperarnte is the sweetish stuff that drips down from or is got from the bark of the river red gum. You find bits of it sitting lined up on the bark and you can also get it after it's dripped to the ground.

ARRERNTE: Ngkwarle aperarnte
ENGLISH: River red gum honeydew
SCIENTIFIC: Eucalyptus camaldu-lensis (river red gum)
The honeydew is produced by small insects.

Ngkwarle aperaltye

Aperaltye apele ineme nhenge walyeke-arleke, apere walyeke-arleke. Lernemele nhenge arlpelhenge atnyerrirretyeke, kalikeweke apeke. Arrwekelenye alakenhe nhenge athirnteke-arle lernewarretyarte imernte arlwilemele. Walyele arlwilemele imernte ikelhe-ilemele, apurte-ilemele. Nhenge atnyerlenge imernte arrernirtnanemele ikelhe.

ARRERNTE: Ngkwarle aperaltye
ENGLISH: River red gum leaf scale
SCIENTIFIC: Eucalyptus camaldulensis (river red gum), Psylla eucalypti (?) (lerp)

River red gum leaf scale

You get small waxy white flakes of aperaltye on the leaves of the river red gum. You shake the branch so that the aperaltye falls from the leaves, onto a sheet or something like that. The people before us used to shake it off onto a flat rock and gather it into little piles. They'd sweep it with a little branch, and pack it into a ball. The bits that fall from the tree are packed into a lump.

ARRERNTE: Ngkwarle alhelpe-arenye
ENGLISH: Mallee spp.
SCIENTIFIC: Eucalyptus spp.(mallee)

Ngkwarle alhelpe-arenye

Ngkwarle alhelpe-arenye apele nhenge, alhelpeke-arleke anteye ineme, alhelpe arlpelheke-arleke anteye. Nhenge aperaltye-arteke anteye arlpelhele aneme. Arne turre-arenye-arle re. Alhelpe-arenye ngkwarle ikwemeye.

Mallee leaf scale

This one is from the mallee bush, from the leaves. It's found on the leaves like aperaltye is. The mallee tree grows on higher ground, and the food you find on its leaves is sweet.

Ngkwarle yerrampe

Ngkwarle yerrampe apele nhenge ahelheke-arle payenteme-ileme, nhenge artetye-artetyele anentye akngerre. Yerre-kenhe alhwenge-arteke arrpenhe ulkere ikwerenhe aneme. Arle akweke-arle arle re. Arle ikwere-ntyele tnyemele ahentye renhe apenteme. Ahentye renhe apentemele imerte kweneke-arle aneme tnyemele angernemele, nhenge itere mapele nhenge ananerle-alperlenge aneme arne inte akwekele tyarre-ineme awantyetyeke. Arlkwenhe-arlkwenhe kwenye-arle yanhe, ware alenyeke-arle arrernemele atnakerte ampinye akakwemele, awantyemele renhe.

ARRERNTE: Ngkwarle yerrampe
ENGLISH: Honeyant
SCIENTIFIC: Melophorus camponotus

Honeyant

The honeyant is found in the ground in mulga country. It's nest is a bit different from other ants' nests. The holes on the surface are small and you dig down from the openings following the shaft. You follow it down, digging and scooping out the dirt. You get the honeyants that are on the side in the main part of the nest, all in a row, and drag them out with a little stick to eat them. You don't swallow them, you put them on your tongue and bite on the abdomen and suck the honey from it.

Ngkwarle arwengalkere Ngkwarle urltampe

Urltampe arrpenhemele atniwemele, kenhe arrpenhemele arwengalkere-arle. Arwengalkere apele nhenge arne akertneke urlpereke areme, alhe akweke apeke nhenge ankere-iperre payenteme-ilemele. Kele renhe atwemele arne tyarrpe-ilemele. Akaperteke-amparre inemele akapertenge-ntyele arreme akweke mape aneme, kele urrknge aneme. Akaperte ampinye akenhe ikelhe arle, akernte-arle-irreke akaperte yanhe arlkwenhe-arlkwenhe anteye, ante nhenge arreme akweke mape mperlkere akweke mape, nhenge akngakeme-arle akaperte renhe, nhenge ngkwarle urrknge-ketye urrke. Urrknge renhe aneme inemele arrerneme urtneke-arleke apeke tyampiteke-arleke apeke, arlkwemele imernte.

Native bee honey

Some people call this urltampe *and others call it* arwengalkere. *You find it up in a hollow in a tree. You find a little 'nose' that's made out of wax sticking out and you chop into the tree and split it open. You get the head part first, where the native bee larvae are, and then the honey. The head part is solid. It's firm and you can eat it too, as well as the little white larvae you get from it. And then you get to the honey itself. You get the honey and put it in a coolamon or a billycan, and then eat it.*

ARRERNTE: Ngkwarle arwengalkere, ngkwarle urltampe
ENGLISH: Native honey, 'sugarbag'

Ngkwarle untyeyampe

Ngkwarle untyeyampe renhe akerle nhenge untarne-untarne mape arlpere-anerlenge. Kele imernte iltyeke-arleke lernemele imernte awantyemele urrperle akweke mape thelelhelenge atnyerrirrerlenge. Arrpenhemele kwatyeke-arleke arrernemele antyweme rlkerte-arle apeke.

Ngkwarle nhenhe-arle apanpele-arle akemele ineme.

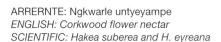

ARRERNTE: Ngkwarle untyeyampe
ENGLISH: Corkwood flower nectar
SCIENTIFIC: Hakea suberea and H. eyreana

Corkwood flower nectar

You get corkwood nectar when the yellow flowers hang down. You shake the nectar onto your hand and lick off the little dark bits that fall there. Sometimes you put it in water and drink it, maybe when you're sick. Everyone collects this food.

Ngkwarle ntewale

Ntewale apele arrkernke-arenye-arle antethe nhenge arrerlkere-akerte. Ntewale ikwere-ntyele nhenge amengele ineme ngkwarle arwengalkere akngerre.

Antethe akemele kwekarerle, renhe iltyeke-arleke lernemele awantyentye akngerre arrerlkere. Ntewale uyerrerlenge arrkirlpangkwerle aneme arrateme.

Bloodwood flower nectar

Ntewale *is the flower of the bloodwood tree which has a pale nectar. Native bees get honey from these flowers. You break off the flower and suck it, or you shake the nectar, which is almost clear, onto your hand and lick it up. When the flowers die off, the bush coconuts* (merne arrkirlpangkwerle) *come out.*

ARRERNTE: Ngkwarle ntewale
ENGLISH: Bloodwood flower nectar
SCIENTIFIC: Eucalyptus opaca

Bloodwood flower illustration by Louise Wellington

MERNE
Food from plants

Merne is foods that are obtained from plants. It includes fruits, the edible leaves, flowers, stems and roots of various plants and edible insect galls found on certain trees.

Merne atwakeye

Merne atwakeye arletye atherrke-
atherrke. Ntyerlenge apeke nhenge
ntyernemerleke-arle atyete anerlenge,
ante kwene renhe arerle untarne-
untarne atherrke-atherrke apeke.
Mwerre akngerre anthurre-arle akemele
ineme nhenge athetheke-athetheke-arle,
alakenhe-arle renhe akemele arlkweme.
Tyerrtye apanpele renhe arlkweme lyete.

ARRERNTE: Merne atwakeye
ENGLISH: Wild orange
SCIENTIFIC: Capparis mitchellii

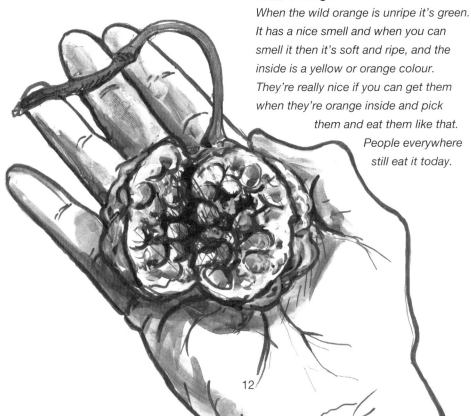

Wild orange

*When the wild orange is unripe it's green.
It has a nice smell and when you can
smell it then it's soft and ripe, and the
inside is a yellow or orange colour.
They're really nice if you can get them
when they're orange inside and pick
them and eat them like that.
People everywhere
still eat it today.*

12

Merne arrutnenge

Merne arrutnenge apele akeme mpenge-irremele, nhenge irrtnye apeke athetheke-athetheke irrerlenge. Mpenge-irreme ante apwernkerlenge annge akweke urrperle mape akenhe akethele anerlenge. Alakenhe renhe mpenge areme arrutnenge. Apmere lhere arrpe-anenhele nhenhe ampinyele lyapeme.

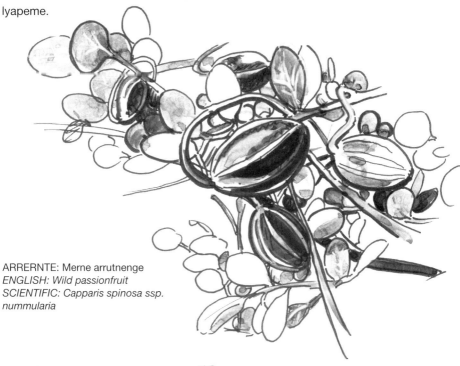

ARRERNTE: Merne arrutnenge
ENGLISH: Wild passionfruit
SCIENTIFIC: Capparis spinosa ssp.
nummularia

Wild passlonfruit

You pick wild passionfruit when it's ripe, when the skin goes orange. When it ripens, it splits open and you can see the little black seeds. That's what it looks like when the wild passionfruit is ripe. It grows in riverbeds all over the place.

13

Merne pmerlpe

Merne pmerlpe apele nhenge irrtnye athetheke-irrerlenge aremele akeme, pmerlpe renhe. Pmerlpe apmere antekerre-antekerre ampinyele lyapeme. Arne pmerlpe arlpentye akngerre ulyentye akngerre-arlke. Merne annge athetheke, ikwerele-arlenge-arle annge lyeke-lyeke akweke kwenele aneme.

Quandong

You pick the quandong fruit when you see it going reddish. The quandong tree grows in the southern part of the Arrernte area. The tree is tall and shady, and the fruit is red and inside it there is a rough seed or stone.

ARRERNTE: Merne pmerlpe
ENGLISH: Quandong
SCIENTIFIC: Santalum acuminatum

Merne utyerrke

Utyerrke mpenge re apele athetheke-irrerlenge akeme. Arrpenhe apele mperlkere-arle arletye-arletye areme. Utyerrke yanhe ulkere urrperle-irremele ingkwelye-irremele, itne ikelhe-ilemele arlkweme. Arne utyerrke re apwerte-apwertele lyapeme, re arne arlarte anthurre aneme.

Wild fig

You pick wild figs when they go red. The white ones you see are unripe. When the fig goes dark and shrivels, they mash them into a ball and eat it. The wild fig tree grows in hilly country and is really bushy.

ARRERNTE: Merne utyerrke
ENGLISH: Wild fig
SCIENTIFIC: Ficus platypoda

Merne mwanyeme

Mwanyeme apele arle awatentye-awatentye lhere iterele lyapentye akngerre. Arlengeke renhe mpenge ntyerneme. Arlele arunthe anthurre arlpere-aneme. Ikwemeye anthurre renhe arlkweme.

Merne awele-awele

Merne awele-awele mpenge apele areme nhenge mperlkere-mperlkere irrerlenge, arrpenheme akenhe athetheke urrperle. Arletye akenhe atherrke-atherrke lterrke-arlke. Mpenge akenhe arlengenge anteye ntyerneme. Nhenge mpenge renhe alpmantheke atyerreme arrernemele kwatyelhe-ilemele, alpmanthele atyerreme. Arrpenhe akenhe ware-arle arlkweme.

Bush tomato

This kind of wild tomato plant is a waxy-looking plant and grows next to creeks. You can smell it from a long way when it's ripe. There are lots of the fruit on each plant. They taste really nice.

Bush tomato

You can see that this type of wild tomato is ripe when you see them go yellowish, or some of them are purplish. When they're unripe, they're green and hard, but you can smell the ripe ones from a long way away. You put the ripe ones in the hot earth by the fire, sprinkle some water on and cover them up to cook, or you can also eat them raw.

ARRERNTE: Merne awele-awele
ENGLISH: Bush tomato
SCIENTIFIC: Solanum ellipticum

ARRERNTE: Merne mwanyeme
ENGLISH: Bush tomato
SCIENTIFIC: Solanum cleistogamum

15

Merne angkwerrpme

Angkwerrpme apele nhenge arne akweke untyeyeke-arleke-arle akeme, ltyentyele apeke anerle. Amare arne arlarte re-arle lyapeme arneke-arleke. Amare ikwerenge lerneme ahelheke atnyerlenge kutyeme. Urrperle arrpenheme athetheke arrpenheme.

EASTERN ARRERNTE:
Merne angkwerrpme
ENGLISH: Mistletoe
SCIENTIFIC: Lysiana exocarpi

Mistletoe

You pick mistletoe berries from a small plant that grows on corkwood or beefwood trees. The mistletoe is a bushy plant that grows right on the tree. You shake the berries from the plant and they fall to the ground and then you can gather them up. Some are dark and others are red.

Merne atyankerne

Merne atyankerne artetyeke-arleke-arle amare aremele, atyankerne lerneme ahelheke tnyetyeke, arleke-arle apeke akemele kwerneme.
Tyerrtye-kenhe merne, ankerre-kenhe, artewe-kenhe, thipe-kenhe.
Arlkwentye akngerre kwenye, alenyeke ikerrke-iwelhentye akngerre.

Mistletoe

You find the atyankerne mistletoe on mulga trees and you shake it so that the fruit fall down to the ground. You can also just pick them off the plant and swallow them. They're food for people, emus, turkeys and other birds. You don't chew them because they stick to your tongue.

ARRERNTE: Merne atyankerne
ENGLISH: Mistletoe
SCIENTIFIC: Amyema preissii

16

Merne pweralheme

Pweralheme akweke arlwe arrpenheme arlpentye-arle arrpenheme. Arne lernelhe-ileme arlperre-arle apeke artetye-arle apeke, arnele atweme amareke ahelheke atnyerrirrerlenge. Yanhe-ulkere ware kwernentye akngerre, akakwetye-akenhe, alenyeke ingkirreke nthirrpmarre-iwelhele.

Mistletoe

Some pweralheme *mistletoe fruit are small and round and others are long. You shake the tree, maybe a whitewood or a mulga, or you hit the mistletoe with a stick and the fruit fall to the ground. Like those other ones* (atyankerne), *you just swallow them without biting them, because then they'll stick to your tongue.*

ARRERNTE: Merne pweralheme
ENGLISH: Mistletoe
SCIENTIFIC: Lysiana sp.

Merne arnweketye
Merne aperlape

Aperlape apele nhenge annge urrperle akweke mape akeme arleke-arleke. Urrperle arrpenheme, arrpenheme athetheke-arle. Ikwemeye anthurre. Arne akweke urtekeke-arle itnenhe akeme. Arne aperlape lyapeme ayerrere itne-arle aknganeke-arle ampinyele, ikngerrele-arlke. Renhe-arle arlkwentye-akngerre kwenye, kwernentye akngerre ware. Ankerrele-arlke kwerneme, artewele-arlke, thipele-arlke. Aperlape-arle arrpenhemele ileme, arrpenhemele arnweketye-arle akeme.

NORTH-EASTERN ARRERNTE: Merne arnweketye
OTHER ARRERNTE: Merne aperlape
ENGLISH: Conkerberry
SCIENTIFIC: Carissa lanceolata

Conkerberry

Conkerberries are small dark fruit which you get from a bush. Some are dark, others are red. They're really sweet. You pick them from a small tree. The conkerberry tree grows in the north, where they came from in the Dreaming, and in the east. You don't chew them, you just swallow them. Emus and bush turkeys and other birds eat them as well.

Some people call them aperlape *and others call them* arnweketye.

Merne arrkirlpangkwerle

Arrkirlpangkwerle apele aneme arrkernkeke-arleke akeme. Apwerteke-arleke-arle arrernemele tyarrpe-ilemele atwemele. Arne kwenele-arle aneme renhe imernte arlkwemele arne akweke tyape angwere-arle renhe ileme. Arrkirlpangkwerle kwenele aneme mperlkere renhe arlkweme-anteye. Arrkernke ahelhe nhenhe ikwerele lyapeme, ahelhele apwerte iterele-arlke. Arne arlarte akngerre, akweke arrpenheme, antethe ikwemeye anthurre ntyerlenge.

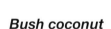

Bush coconut

You get these insect galls that are called bush coconuts on the bloodwood tree. You put one on a rock and hit it to split it open. The little insect, which is found inside, and which is called angure, *is eaten. The white flesh of the coconut is also eaten. Bloodwood trees grow throughout this area on flat ground and at the foot of hills. The tree can be large and bushy or small, and has sweet smelling flowers.*

ARRERNTE: Merne arrkirlpangkwerle
ENGLISH: Bush coconut
SCIENTIFIC: Eucalyptus opaca (bloodwood tree), Cysticoccus pomiformis (insect in gall)

Merne alangkwe
Merne ulkantyerrknge
Merne altyeye

Merne alangkwe apele nhenge akngerre arlkweme ante akweke. Akweke renhe akenhe amwerterrpe-arle akeme, antethe renhe-arle akenhe ileme ulkantyerrknge. Altyeye arlkweme anteye. Itne aneme ikelhe-ikelhe akweke mape-arle. Alangkwe arrpenheme nhenge alpmanthele atyerremele, arrpenhe mape akenhe arletye-anteye apeke arlkwerlenge akwerrke. Artekerre renhe atnetye-arle ileme, renhe arlkweme arlotye apeke mpenge apeke.

ARRERNTE: Merne alangkwe, merne ulkantyerrknge, merne altyeye
ENGLISH: Bush banana fruit, flower and leaves
SCIENTIFIC: Marsdenia australis

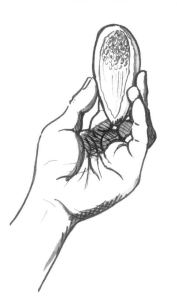

Bush banana fruit
Bush banana flower
Bush banana leaves

You can eat bush bananas (alangkwe) when they are small or full-grown. The small fruits are called amwerterrpe and the flowers are called ulkantyerrknge. These flowers hang in clusters and can also be eaten. You can even eat the plant (which is called altyeye) itself. You can cook bush bananas in hot earth, or they can be eaten raw when they are young. The root of the plant is called atnetye and it can also be eaten raw or cooked.

Merne atnetye

Arrpenhe akenhe atnetye-arle nhenge altyeye-iperre yanhe arle. Mperlkere anthurre atyerremele, atyerremele alpmanthele arlkwerle. Arrinketyeke arlkwenhe-arlkwenhe.

Bush banana root

Another food is the root of the bush banana plant. You cook up these really white ones in hot dirt and eat them. It gives you a good appetite when you eat it.

ARRERNTE: Merne atnetye
ENGLISH: Bush banana root
SCIENTIFIC: Marsdenia australis

Merne ataltyakwerle

Merne arrpenhe akenhe ataltyakwerle nhenge artetye walyeke-arleke akenhe-akenhe-arle. Artetye arne itereke inentye akngerre-arle, arntarlkwe akantyele anirtnerlenge. Alpmanthele atyerrentye akngerre arrpenhe, arrpenheme akenhe arletye ware-arle arlkwerlenge. Artetye arrpe-anenhele itne aneme apmere nhenhe ikwere. Artetye ahelhele apwerte iterele-arlke lyapeme.

ARRERNTE: Merne ataltyakwerle
ENGLISH: Mulga apples (insect gall)
SCIENTIFIC: Acacia aneura (tree)

Mulga apple

Another food is the mulga apple which is got from the mulga. The mulga apples grow along the ends of the branches. You can eat them raw or after cooking in hot earth. Mulga apples are found on mulga trees all over this area. The trees grow in flat country and at the foot of hills.

Merne arrankweye

Merne arrankweye apele nhenge apwerte iterele lhere ntyerele arlke lyapeme apmere apanpe nhenhele. Annge urrperle-arle ikwerenge arrateme, antethe mperlkere akweke. Annge arunthe anthurre arlpere aneme arnele-arlenge, arne pmwelkerele-arlenge, annge akweke-arle kwenele aneme-akerte.

Bush plum

Bush plums grow at the foot of hills and in floodout areas all over this region. It has dark fruit and small white flowers. Lots of the fruit, which has small seeds inside, hang from the branches of the tree, which are blue-grey.

ARRERNTE: Merne arrankweye
ENGLISH: Bush plums
SCIENTIFIC: Carissa lanceolata

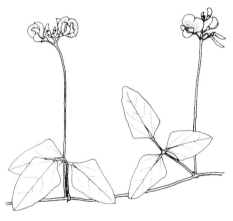

Merne arlatyeye

Merne arlatyeye apele nhenge lhereke-arle tnyeme, arlpentye akngerre. Mperlkere-arle renhe tnyeme. Alpmanthele iteme akernte-arle akenhe re irrerlenge. Arrpenheme akngerre, arrpenheme akenhe utyewe arlpentye.

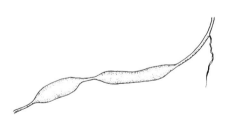

ARRERNTE: Merne arlatyeye
ENGLISH: Pencil yams
SCIENTIFIC: Carissa lanceolata

Pencil yam

You dig up pencil yams, the long ones, in creekbeds. They're white when you dig them up. You cook them in hot soil until they are just firm. Some are big and fat and others are long and thin.

Illustrations on this page by Jenny Green and Felicity Green

Merne yalke

Merne yalke apele nhenge turreke-arle
tnyeme name antyerrke-irrerlenge
inemele. Antyerrke-irrerlenge merne yalke
annge aneme. Tnyemele aneme ineme,
irrtnye-iwemele akenhe arlkweme.

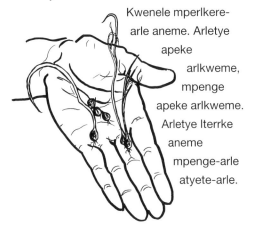

Kwenele mperlkere-
arle aneme. Arletye
apeke
arlkweme,
mpenge
apeke arlkweme.
Arletye lterrke
aneme
mpenge-arle
atyete-arle.

Wild onion

*You dig up wild onions from
the creek bank when the
grass of the plant has dried
out. When it has dried
out, the wild onion bulb
is ready. Then you
dig it up, husk it
and eat it. It's
white on the
inside and
you can eat
it raw or
cooked. It's hard
when it's raw but soft when it's cooked.*

ARRERNTE: Merne yalke
ENGLISH: Wild onions
SCIENTIFIC: Cyperus bulbosus

Merne ilkwarte

Ilkwarte re akenhe nhenge cucumber-
arteke, akweke, annge-akerte. Mpenge
akenhe mperlkere-irreme, ikwemeye
anthurre. Arunthe anthurre arle anyentele
aneme. Lherele, turrele, ntyerele itne
lyapeme.

Bush cucumber

Ilkwarte *is like a
cucumber, it's
small and has
seeds. When it's
ripe, it goes white. It's
really tasty. You get a lot of them on one
plant. They grow in creeks,
riverbanks and floodout areas.*

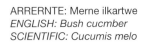

ARRERNTE: Merne ilkartwe
ENGLISH: Bush cucmber
SCIENTIFIC: Cucumis melo

Merne ayepe

Merne ayepe yanhe-arle arlatyeye-arteke itenhe-itenhe. Alpmanthele atyerrerlenge akernte-irreme. Ayepe-arenyele ayepe arlpelhe arlkweme. Ayepe renhe rapitele arlkweme artekerre tnyemele.

ARRERNTE: Merne ayepe
ENGLISH: Tar vine
SCIENTIFIC: Boerhavia coccinea

Tar vine

The root of the tar vine is cooked like the arlatyeye yam, cooked in hot soil until it's just firm. Ayepe-arenye caterpillars eat the leaves of the plant, and rabbits dig up the roots and eat them.

Merne anatye

Anatye apele nhenge arle akngerreke-arleke tnyeme ahelhe urrpereke. Akngerre-apenhe anthurre imernte tyerremele, alpmanthele atyerremele arlkwerle. Akwerrke akenhe atyete anthurre arle. Atningkele-ante apeke anatye renhe arlkwerle anyente akngerre-apenhe apeke.

Bush potato

You dig for bush potatoes in the cracks around this large plant. Then you pull out the big root thing and cook it in hot earth and eat it. The little ones are really soft, and if it's a big one, it will feed a lot of people.

ARRERNTE: Merne anatye
ENGLISH: Bush potato
SCIENTIFIC: Ipomoea costata

Merne akatyerre

Akatyerre apele ahelhele urure-wemele ineme mpenge-irrerlenge. Nhenge untarne-untarne itne aneme kwarte-arle itne ileme, kenhe ingkwelye-arle-irreme merne akatyerre itnenhe akemele ikelhe-ilemele arlkweme. Arrpenheme akenhe arlenge-ntyele ware akemele arlkwerlenge.

Bush sultana

When bush sultanas ripen, you get them and rub them with sand in your hands (to get the furry stuff off the skin). They call the yellow ones eggs. When they start to shrivel up, you pick them and pack them together and eat them, or sometimes you just pick them and eat them straight from the plant.

ARRERNTE: Merne akatyerre
ENGLISH: Bush sultanas
SCIENTIFIC: Solanum centrale

MERNE NTANGE
Edible seeds

Ntange is edible seeds, and because it is food from
a plant, it is also a type of *merne*.

Merne ntange ulyawe

Ntange ulyawe apele nhenge arle
akweke urtekeke-arleke ineme. Urrknge-
ilemele renhe athemele imerte
nhenge thelelhetyeke impemele
arrpenhe ampinye-werne, ante
imerte awantyemele arrpenheme
ikelhe-arle-ileme arlkwetyeke.

Pigweed seed

*You get these edible seeds from a short
little plant (pigweed). You mash them up
on a grinding stone and leave it for the
juice to drain to one side of the stone.
You lick up the juice and make the seed
pulp into a patty and eat it.*

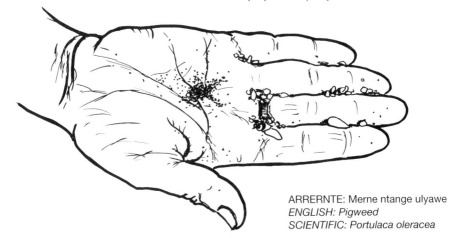

ARRERNTE: Merne ntange ulyawe
ENGLISH: Pigweed
SCIENTIFIC: Portulaca oleracea

Merne ntange arlepe

Ntange arlepe apele nhenge irrtnye arletye anerlenge akerle alpmanthele atyerremele arlkwerle. Arrpenheme akenhe antyerrke-irrerlenge ineme, urrperle akweke mape. Ahelheke akenhe nhenge atnyeke-arle inemele antime urtneke-arleke arrernemele. Nhenge arne alparreke-arleke arrernemele imernte anthelke uthene renhe uthene akngakemele. Kele akngakeke-arle-iperre aneme alpmantheke arrerneme atyerretyeke. Arletye-arlke arlkweme.

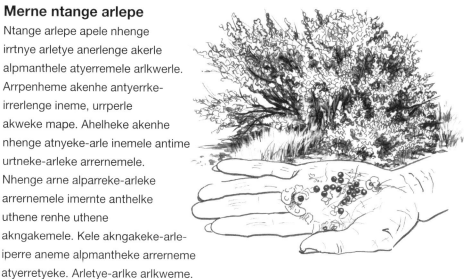

Prickly wattle seed

You get the prickly wattle seed pods when they are green and cook them in hot earth and eat them. You can collect them when they have started to dry out, the little dark ones. You collect the ones that have fallen onto the ground in a coolamon. You put them in a long coolamon and winnow them to separate the seeds from the rubbish. When you've separated them out you put them in the hot earth to cook. You can also eat them raw.

ARRERNTE: Merne ntange arlepe
ENGLISH: Prickly wattle seed
SCIENTIFIC: Acacia victoriae

Merne ntange artetye

Ntange artetye renhe apele urtneke-arleke arrerneme, atherrke anteye akemele urrpme akerte, atyerretyeke aneme arlkwetyenhele. Arletye apeke mpenge apeke arlkweme.

ARRERNTE: Merne ntange artetye
ENGLISH: Mulga seeds
SCIENTIFIC: Acacia aneura

Mulga seeds

You collect mulga seeds in a coolamon. You pick them while the seed pods are still green and rippled, and cook them and eat them. You can eat them raw as well as cooked.

Merne ntange arlketyerre

Ntange arlketyerre apele nhenge urrpme atherrke-atherrke arrpenheme anerlenge, atherrke anteye-arle, arrpenheme akenhe athetheke-athetheke. Urrpme renhe ware rarle aremele akirtnanemele mwerre ulkere mpenge-ilemele atyerremele arlkweme. Arlketyerre urrpmenge tyerremele arlkweme.

Dead finish seed

Some of the seedpods from the dead finish tree are greenish, but still green, and others are reddish. When you see the seed pod is ripe you pick them one after another and then cook them in the hot earth and eat them. You get the seeds out of the rippled seedpod to eat them.

ARRERNTE: Merne ntange arlketyerre
ENGLISH: Dead finish seed
SCIENTIFIC: Acacia tetragonophylla

TYAPE
Edible grubs, caterpillars and other insects

Tyape are edible grubs, caterpillars or other insects.
The grubs, which are mostly the larvae of different
types of moths, are a fairly popular food but caterpillars
and other insects are not eaten very often these days.
The common Australian English term 'witchetty grub' is
usually used to refer to any type of edible grub, but this
should not be confused with the particular type of grub
found in the roots of the witchetty bush, *atnyematye*.

Tyape atnyematye

Tyape atnyematye apele tyape arle yanhe nhenge atnyeme-arenye-arle. Ahelhe urrpereke-arle aremele tnyemele. Artekerre arlware-arle-irreke arwakemele tyerrerle. Alpmanthele atyerremele imernte arlkwemele; arletye apeke arlkwemele, mpenge apeke. Tyape atnyematye atnulkele utyene apernelhenhe, arnteme-arle apernelhenhe, nhenge rlkerte-arle awelheme.

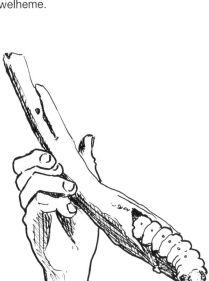

Witchetty grub

Atnyematye is the edible grub from the witchetty bush. You find cracks in the ground and then dig there. You lever up the root which is swollen because of the grub inside, and break it and pull the grub out. You can eat it raw or cook it in hot earth and then eat it. You can put the guts from the grub on sores, where you've got a pain, or when you're feeling sick.

ARRERNTE: Tyape atnyematye
ENGLISH: Witchetty grub
SCIENTIFIC: Xyleutes leucomochla

30

Tyape ahernenge
Tyape ahekwene

Tyape ahernenge
akenhe apere
artekerrele-arle aneme. Apere
artekerrele, arlpentye
akngerre ahentye
tnetye-akerleme,
artekerre arrpenhe-werne
arrateme tyape ikwere-werle
atheke. Tyape ahekwene
tyerreme name
tunpere arlpentye
akwernemele tyarre-ineme, iparrpe
anthurre tyerreme tunpere ikwerele.
Akngerre-apenhe mperlkere, ure
alpmanthele atyerremele arlkweme tyape
arrpenhe areye arteke anteye. Tyape
ahernenge intentye akngerre
ahentye urrperle nhenge renhe
areme arnkarre itere
akethelhe-ilerlenge kwatye
urewele apere artekerre atnartenge
apeke. Akartwe ahelhe turreke areme.

River red gum grub

The ahernenge *grub lives
in the roots of the river
red gum tree. A long tube
leads down from the
surface to the root where
the grub is. You pull the
grub out by putting a long
piece of hooked grass down
the shaft and pulling the grub out
very quickly. It's a big white one and
you cook it in the hot earth and eat
it the same as other grubs. The
tubes where the* ahernenge *lives are
black and you can see them on the roots
of gumtrees in the creek bank when
they've been exposed by floodwaters.
The little lid on the tube can
be seen on the high
ground next to the
creek.*

NORTH-EASTERN ARRERNTE: Tyape ahekwene
OTHER EASTERN ARRERNTE: Tyape ahernenge
ENGLISH: *River red gum grub*
SCIENTIFIC: *Trictena argentata*

Tyape ingwenenge

Ingwenenge apele tyape nhenge aperele-
arle aneme-arle. Mperlkere, artepe
akenhe intelhentye urrperle-urrperle.
Apereke-arleke ilepele atwemele
akngerre-apenhe anthurre tyerreme
tunperele. Tunpere re akenhe arne name
lhere-arenye-ntyele mpwareke arle.
Alpmanthele atyerremele yanhe renhe
arlkweme. Arletye-arlke arlkweme.

River red gum grub

Ingwenenge *is the edible grub that lives in
red gums. It's white with purplish marks
across its back. You chop into the tree
with an axe and use a grass hook to pull
out a big, fat one. The grass hook is made
from a type of long grass that is found in
creeks. You cook the grub in hot earth
and eat it. You can also eat it raw.*

ARRERNTE: Tyape ingwenenge
ENGLISH: *River red gum grub*
SCIENTIFIC: *Possibly Trictena argentata*

Tyape ankerrutne

Ankerrutne renhe apele ankerreke-arle ineme, mperlkere anthurre arle re-akenhe, akngerre-apenhe. Re ingwenenge-arteke arle waneye ankerre-arenye arle. Apere ankerrenge tunperele tyerreme. Renhe alpmanthele atyerremele antime renhe arlkwenhe-arlkwenhe.

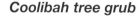

Coolibah tree grub

You get ankerrutne *grubs from the coolibah tree. They're large and really white. It looks like the grub from the river red gum, only it lives in the coolibah. You pull it out of the tree with a grass hook and cook it in hot earth and then eat it.*

ARRERNTE: Tyape ankerrutne
ENGLISH: Coolibah tree grub
SCIENTIFIC: Eucalyptus sp. (tree)

Tyape arlperrayte

Tyape arlperrayte akenhe akaperte akngerre arle, arne lyarrtyeke-arleke renhe ineme, arlperre antyerrke arle irreke-arleke artekerre kweneke. Arne atnyeke-arleke tnyemele arwakemele tyerreme artekerreke-arlke ineme. Renhe arlkwentye akngerre alpmanthele atyerremele tyape arrpenheme arteke anteye arle.

Whitewood tree grub

The edible grub from the whitewood tree has a big head, and you get it from inside the roots of the trees, when the trees are dead and dried out. You dig out the base of the fallen tree and lever it up to pull it out. Then you get the grubs out of the roots. You cook them in hot earth and eat them just like other edible grubs.

NORTH-EASTERN ARRERNTE: Tyape arlperrayte
ENGLISH: Whitewood tree grub
SCIENTIFIC: Atalaya hemiglauca (tree)
Possibly Cerambycidaea family (grub)

.Tyape athengayte

Tyape athengayte
athenge artekerrele
anenhe-anenhe, renhe
alpmanthele
atyerremele arlkwentye
akngerre. Alpmantholo ante
ware itenhe-itenhe lterrke-
irretyeke tyape mape kwene atyete
arle itne. Tyape arlperre-arenye arteke
renhe areme antere akngerre-arle

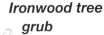

Ironwood tree grub

Athengayte *lives
in the roots of the
ironwood tree. You
cook it up in hot soil and
eat it. You cook it until it's
crisp on the outside and
soft on the inside. They look
like the whitewood grubs,
only they're fatter.*

NORTH-EASTERN ARRERNTE: Tyape athengayte
ENGLISH: Ironwood tree grub
SCIENTIFIC: Acacia estropholiata (tree)

Tyape arlepayte

Tyape arlepe-arenye
akenhe atnyematye-
arteke mperlkere.
Arlepe ikwerele-arlenge
tyape atherrame aneme:
arlepayte, arrpenhe
akenhe akweke, arlperre-
arenye-arteke, arne
atnartengele aneme.
Akaperte ultakemele arrernemele
apernelhenhelhenhe, arelhe nhenge
werlatye alhe apernelhenhelhenhe,
utyene arrpenheme-arlke. Artekerre-
arenye arlkwenhe-
arlkwenhe. Renhe iteme
alpmanthele atyerremele
arlkweme tyape arrpenhe
areye arteke.

Prickly wattle grub

*One type of grub found
on the prickly wattle grub
is white like a witchetty
grub. There are two
sorts of grub in the
prickly wattle: the edible
arlepayte and this
other one, which is
smaller. It is like the grub from the
whitewood tree, because it lives in
the base of the tree. You break off the
head (and squeeze the insides) onto a
sore and rub it in. Women put it on sore
nipples, and it's used for other sores, too.
The one from the root is eaten. You cook
them in hot earth and eat them like other
grubs.*

NORTH-EASTERN ARRERNTE: Tyape arlepayte
ENGLISH: Prickly wattle grub
SCIENTIFIC: Acacia victoriae (tree)

Tyape tyerraye

Tyape tyerraye arrwekelenye mapele arlkwerrirretyarte. Ahelheke tnyemele, ahelhe turreke, arnkarreke. Altywere ikwerenhe inurle-kenhe alhwenge-arteke. Akwerrke teke-anerlenge irrarlenge arrateke-arle arrpenhe akenhe alhwengeke irrarle-akerte ineme. Arrwekele arrpenhemele arlkwerrirretyarte arletye, mpenge ure aperrkeke-arleke iwemele arlkwerle.

Cicadas

In the past, people used to eat cicadas. They'd dig them out of the ground, from the high ground next to creeks, or from the banks. Their holes are like spiders' holes. People would catch them when they were drying off after shedding their shell, or sometimes from the ground when they were still in their shells. They used to eat them raw or cooked. They'd toss them on the coals and then eat them.

ARRERNTE: Tyape tyerraye
ENGLISH: Cicadas
SCIENTIFIC: Thopha saccata

Tyape ntyarlke

Tyape ntyarlke tyape ayepe-arenye-arteke kenhe tyape ayepe-arenyenge akngerre ulkere. Renhe atneltyeme tyape ayepe-arenye-arteke anteye. Tyape ntyarlke ayepeke-arleke atherrke turrele lyapemeke-arleke ineme, renhe atyerreme tyape ayepe-arenye arteke anteye. Alakenhe renhe arrwekelenyele arlkwerrirretyarte.

Elephant grub

The elephant grub (caterpillar) is like the ayepe-arenye *but it's bigger. You squeeze the guts out like you do with the* ayepe-arenye. Ntyarlke *is found on the tarvine and on grass that grows on the high ground next to creeks. You cook it like* ayepe-arenye. *That's how people used to eat it before.*

ARRERNTE: Tyape ntyarlke
SCIENTIFIC: Elephant grub caterpillar

Tyape ayepe-arenye

Tyape ayepe-arenye ayepeke-arleke ineme. Arrwekelenyele utnhetyarte ayepe arlkwerlenge inemele, ahelheke arrernemele atneltyele ahelhe iperte-werle atheke. Ikwerenge arrernemele ure alpmanthele atyerremele. Tyerremale-iperre teke-iwemele antyerrke-irretyeke, uneke atherrele apeke urrpetyele apeke, awethe ulkere apeke. Arrpenhemele-arlke anthemele arlkwetyeke.

Tar vine caterpillars

You get ayepe-arenye *caterpillars on the tar vine. Before, people used to gather them while the caterpillars were eating the plant. They would put the* ayepe-arenye *on the ground and squeeze the guts out into a little hole, and then cook the caterpillars in hot soil. Then they get them out and leave them in the sun for two or three days, or longer, to dry. Then they'd share them around and eat them.*

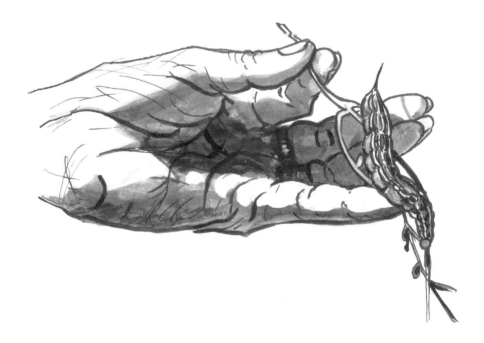

ARRERNTE: Tyape ayepe-arenye
ENGLISH: Tar vine caterpillars
SCIENTIFIC: Celerio lineata livornicoides

Tyape utnerrengatye

Tyape utnerrengatye akenhe
utnerrengeke-arlke areme. Utnerrengeke-
arleke arlwilemele urtneke-arleke,
tyampiteke arrernemele. Utnerrenge
arnele-arlenge anerlenge anpeme arne
itne ingkerreke anthurre arrurelheme
ahelhe-werle. Tyape arrpenhe yanhe
atherre arteke anteye atyerremele
arlkwerle, ayepe-arenye uthene ntyarlke
uthene arteke.

Emu bush grub

The utnerrengatye *grub is found on the
emu bush. You gather them up into a
coolamon or tin. If you touch the tree
when the grubs are sitting on it, they all
fall off onto the ground. You cook them
and eat them like the other two grubs,*
ayepe-arenye *and* ntyarlke.

ARRERNTE: Tyape utnerrengatye
ENGLISH: Emu bush grub
SCIENTIFIC: Eremophila freelingii (tree)

KERE
Meat and other food from animals

Kere is food from animals, especially meat. It is also used in describing other foods from animals such as fat, eggs, blood, intestines and other parts. Cheese, which is not a traditional food, can be referred to as *'kere* cheese'. Animals which are sources of food can also be described as *kere*.

Kere arlewatyerre

Kere arlewatyerre nhenge ahelheke arle
atweme, arrpenheme arneke-arle.
Itetyeke akenhe ntheke-iwemele
alkngenthele irrtnyeke-amparre
ampetyeke tiwemele imernte atyerremele
alpmanthele ane aperrkele aneme,
akertneke arrernemele, mpenge-
irretyenhenge. Arrpenheme kwarte-arle
atnertele aneme akerte ulperre
athenemele atyerremele iteme, kwarte
ateketye.

Kere arlewatyerre athetheke-athetheke,
arlewatyerre urreye arlpentye-arlpentye
marle akngerre ulkere. Ahelhe urrkalele,
lherele apeke, turrele apeke, alhwengele
ikwerenhe anenhe-anenhe, alhwenge
angkweye arrpenhemele arlke. Kere
nhenhe ahelhe apanpele atwemele
arlkwenhe-arlkwenhe.

Goanna

*You catch goannas on the ground or in
trees. To cook them, you just toss them
on the flames to singe the skin, and then
cook them in the ashes and coals, putting
them on top. If it has eggs in its stomach,
you lay it down on its stomach to cook,
so that the eggs don't burst.*

*This goanna is an orangey colour. The
males are fairly long and the females are
shorter and thicker. They live in flat red
sand country, or in creeks, or on the
banks, in their own burrows or in ones
left by other animals. People all over this
region catch and eat these goannas.*

ARRERNTE: Kere arlewatyerre
ENGLISH: Gould's sand goanna
SCIENTIFIC: Varanus gouldii

Kere ulkerte
Kere atyunpe

Ulkerte uthene atyunpe uthene arrirtne
anyente re. Kere ulkerte akenhe arneke
atweme, alhwengeke apeke, unthele-
anerlenge. Terteke arlke unthenhe-
unthenhe. Untye renhe atwetyeke ante
urtethe. Atweke-arle iperre imernte kele
renhe atne-ite inemele arrakertenge,
kenhe atne arrpenhe akenhe atnilhenge
atne-tye ineme, tyerreme akenhe.

Renhe ntheke-iwemele, tiwemele, kele
imernte ingke atherreke interlpe
arrernemele tile athnwerte-ilemele
arrernenhe. Alpmanthe akngerrele renhe
atyerreme aperrkinpe-aperrkinpele-arle
arterle mpenge-irretyeke.

Ulkerte-arle atyerreme,
arlewatyerre-arle
atyerreme-arteke
anteye.

Kere akngerre-apenhe
anthurre, arlpentye anthurre
ankertenge-arlke arlewatyerrenge-arlke.
Akngerre arle re, nterlpenternentye
akngerre.

Alhwenge apwerte iterele anemele,
rapite-kenhe alhwengele, lhereke-arlke,
turreke-arlke.

Perentie

Ulkerte *and* atyunpe *mean the same
thing, a perentie lizard. You catch
perenties in a tree or in a burrow or
walking around. They wander around
when it's wet. You hit them on the back of
the head or the lower back, and when
you've killed it you pull some of its guts
out through the mouth and other guts out
through the backside.
You singe the perentie on the fire (to get
the skin off). Then you join the legs
together in pairs with wooden skewers
and fold the tale under and cook it in a lot
of hot soil (from a fire), covering it with dirt
and coals,
until it's*

*cooked. Perenties and
goannas are cooked in
the same way.
Perenties are a large
animal, much longer than a
bearded dragon or a goanna.
They're big and spotted.
They live in burrows on the
sides of hills, in old
rabbit burrows, in
creeks or on
the banks.*

NORTH-EASTERN ARRERNTE: Kere ulkerte
OTHER EASTERN ARRERNTE: Kere atyunpe
ENGLISH: Perentie
SCIENTIFIC: Varanus giganteus

Kere amwelye
Kere ankerte

Kere amwelye atweme arne antyerrkele tnerlenge. Unte urrperle-urrperleke-amparre renhe atwerle, kele ilweke-arle imernte athetheke-athetheke anteme renhe aremele. Kele renhe atwetye-akenhe-arle renhe akaperte ware arle renhe akakweme imernte ntewemele ahelheke-arleke apeke arneke-arleke apeke. Arrwekelenye mapele akaperte ware akakwetyarte.

Ntheke-iwemele tiwemele atyerremele. Arralkerlenge iltye irrpetyale alknge ante pwenge-irrentye akngerre artitye lterrke-irreme.

Bearded dragon

You catch bearded dragons when they're sitting in dead trees. They're grey, at first, when you kill them, but when they've been dead for a bit they go orange. You don't just hit them, you bite them on the back of the neck and then smash them against a tree or the ground. The people before us used to just bite the head.

You lightly cook them to singe the skin off then cook them in hot soil. If the mouth is open, don't put your finger in because they'll close their eyes and clamp their jaws shut.

EASTERN ARRERNTE: Kere amwelye
CENTRAL ARRERNTE: Kere ankerte
ENGLISH: Bearded dragon
SCIENTIFIC: Pogona vitticeps

Kere kaperle
Kere kelyawe

Kere kelyawe apele nhenhe arenye mapele atniweme kenhe anwerne kaperle-arle atniweme. Kelyawe arne antyerrkele tnerlenge, turrele, ahelhele-arlke. Ureke ntheke-iwemele iteme. Ampele arlkwenhe-arlkwenhe, antere akngerre anteye. Ampe akweke mapele kwarte arlke arlkwenhe-arlkwenhe.

Dragon lizard

Alice Springs people call the dragon lizard kelyawe but we call it kaperle. They live in dead trees, on the high ground next to creeks and on flat ground too. You singe the skin first then cook them. Dragon lizards have got a lot of fat in them and kids eat them. Kids eat the eggs too.

EASTERN ARRERNTE: Kere kaperle
CENTRAL ARRERNTE: Kere kelyawe
ENGLISH: Dragon lizard
SCIENTIFIC: Agamidae spp.

Kere arntetherrke

Kere arrpenhe akenhe arntetherrke-arle.
Apwerte athirntele anenhe-anenhe,
akngerre-apenhe anthurre ahe-akngerre
kwenye. Kere arlkwenhe-arlkwenhe
apmwe. Apere urlteke atweme, alhwenge
arriweke teke-anerlenge alhwerrpeke.
'Alhe-ilperre' arle renhe itne atniweme.
Renhe alpmanthele atyerreme, ntheke-
iweme. Kele artepe imernte akemele
aletye arratyentye artepe ayenpe
itepe-itere atherre akantyeke-
atwetye aketye-akerleme nhenge
ntheke-arle-iweke iperrele antere
alekelye. Kele renhe lyamle-
ilemele alpmanthele atyerreme.
Mpenge-irrerlenge akeme artepe
akeke-arle ikwerenge anteye,
tyarrpe-ilemele. Atningke anthurrele
arlkwentye akngerre.

Carpet snake

*Another animal you can eat
is the carpet snake. It lives
on flat rocks and is very
big but it's not aggressive.
It's an edible snake. You
catch it in a hollow in a tree
or in the opening of its burrow
when it warms itself in the sun in
winter. People call it 'flat-nose' too.
You cook it in hot earth but singe it
first to get the scales off. You put two
straight
cuts in the skin on the
back either side of the
spine all the way to the tip of
the tail so that the fat won't
burst out after the skin is
singed. Then you coil the snake
up and cook it in hot soil. When
it's ready, you slice down the back
where you cut it before to split it open. It
feeds a lot of people.*

ARRERNTE: Kere arntetherrke
ENGLISH: Carpet snake
SCIENTIFIC: *Morelia bredli*

Kere aherre

Kere aherre apele nhenge ahelheke arerle, urrkaleke, Irrtyartele arrwekele atanthewarretyarte, akngwelyele ipernerle. Lyete ulkere akenhe makitele ante aneme atyerrewarreparreme. Atyerremele apeke, nternemele apeke atninerle. Lyepe-lyepe tyerremele interlpe arrernemele. Kele ure alkngentheke ntheke-iwemele, tiwemele, atyerremele, arlpele uthene aperrkele uthene. Tile ultakerle, ingke atherre ultakerle, atyerrerle, tile uthene ingke uthene ikwere-arleke anteye anyentelhe-ilemele atyerreme.

ARRERNTE: Kere aherre
ENGLISH: Kangaroo
SCIENTIFIC: Macropus rufus

Kangaroo

You find kangaroos in flat country or mulga country. In the old days, people used to sool their dogs on them and spear them. Nowadays, people shoot them with guns. They shoot them or spear them and then gut them. The milk guts are pulled out and a wooden skewer is used to close up the carcase. Then it's tossed on top of a fire to singe the hair which is scraped off, and then it's (put in a hole and) covered up with hot earth and coals to cook it. The tail and both feet are cut off before cooking. These are put in together with the rest of the carcase.

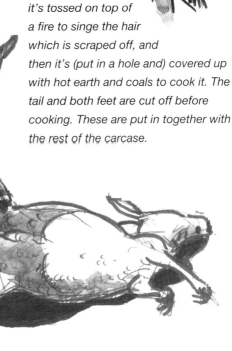

Tyipe-arle-ileme arunthele arlkwetyeke.
Ulyepere-iperre awerrpe antyweme, ulte-
iperre uthene. Kere aherre mwerrantye
tyipe-ilenhe-ilenhe; ulyepere atherre,
anenye atherre, ulte atherre, atnerte,
akaperte, tile, ingke atherre, artepe,
urtethe. Alakenhe renhe apanpele tyipe-
llerreme, Arrerntele.

*The kangaroo is chopped up so that a lot
of people can eat it. The warm blood and
fluids from the thighs and the hollow of
the chest are drunk. Kangaroos are cut
up in a special way; into the two thighs,
the two hips, the two sides of ribs, the
stomach, the head, the tail, the two feet,
the back and the lower back. This is the
way that Arrernte people everywhere cut
it up.*

Kere arrwe

Arrwe renhe areme atwetye akweke
arteke. Arrwe apele apwertele anentye
akngerre, apwerte tyarrpele re aneme
lyerlele. Yanhe ulkere atne-inemele
ntheke-arlke-iwemele, tile arlke. Kele
imernte ure alkngentheke-arleke ntheke-
arlke-iwemele, alpmanthele atyerremele.
Ingke ultakemele, tile arlke, ingkerreke
anyente-ilemele
alpmanthe iperteke
atyerremele,
ahelhe alpmanthe
arrernemele,
aperrke akweke
ware arrerneme,
kele ahelhe arletye
arrernemele.

Rock wallaby

*Rock wallabies look like little kangaroo
joeys. They live on hills, on the gravelly
sand in the gaps between the rocks. Like
the kangaroo, you gut them and singe
them on the fire, with the tail, and then
cook them in hot soil. You cut off the feet
and the tail and put everything in together
in a pit of hot earth. Then you put more
hot earth and some coals on top, and
then some cool earth on top of that and
then leave it to cook.*

ARRERNTE: Kere arrwe
ENGLISH: Rock wallaby
SCIENTIFIC: Petrogale lateralis

Kere arenge

Kere arenge apele apwertele anentye
akngerre-arle. Renhe aherre arle iteme
arteke anteye, atninemele, lyepe-lyepe
uthene anthwerrke uthene tyerremele,
interlpe arrernemele, ureke ntheke-
iwemele, lterre atherre
ultakemele, tile ultakemele,
ingkerreke anthurre imernte
itne ampemele. Mpenge-
irrerlenge tyerreme tyipe-
ileme. Ulyepere
atherre-ntyele
awerrpe
antyweme, ulte-
iperre arlke.

Euro

*The euro lives in the hills. You cook it like
you cook a kangaroo; gut it, pull out the
milk guts and the other guts,
close it up with a wooden skewer
and then singe it on the fire.
Then you cut off both the feet
and the tail and cook them all
together. When it's cooked, you
pull it out and cut it up. You can
drink the warm blood from the
thighs and the side.*

ARRERNTE: Kere arenge
ENGLISH: Euro
SCIENTIFIC: Macropus robustus

44

Kere antenhe

Kere antenhe akenhe nhenge
atnyentyeke atwenhe-atwenhe-arle,
urlteke arlke apeke atwerle. Atne-
inemele, interlpe arrernemele, ntheke-
iwemele atyerrerle, alpmanthele anteye.
Ntewale-iperre ikwemeye anthurre renhe
arlkweme kere lyepe-lyepe arlke. Kere
antenhe kwenhe arrwekelenye akngerre
aneke, lyete ulkere akenhe anyente-ame-
anyente ahelhe nhenhele aneme.

Possum

*You catch possums by moonlight (when
they move around) or when they're in
their holes in trees. You gut them, close
them up with a wooden skewer, singe the
fur off and then cook them in hot soil.
When you eat them after they have been
eating nectar from bloodwood trees, they
taste really sweet, especially the milk
guts. There used to be lots of possums,
but nowadays they are few and far
between.*

ARRERNTE: Kere antenhe
ENGLISH: Possum
SCIENTIFIC: Trichosurus vulpecula

Kere inape

Kere inape akenhe apwerte altyartweke-
arleke atwenhe-atwenhe, arne ulpereke
arleke apeke inerle, alhwenge
arnkwerrkngeke apeke. Re akenhe lyeke
akngerre-arle, inwenge-arle renhe
atweme tnyilemele. Atne-ineme atnerte
mpepe, lyepe-lyepe tyerremele interlpe
arrernemele.

Kele ure aperrkeke iperte-ilemele imernte
artepe arrernemele akertneke. Re akenhe
kwene ipertele anerlenge, aperrke uthene
alpmanthe uthene lyeke ikwere-arleke
arrernemele, lyeke mape imernte
arrpetyenhele. Renhe ilepele apeke itne
arrpeme kanyengarrele apeke, pmware
mpwarenharenhe nhengele ulkere. Kele
lyeke ingkerreke irlwekenge alpmanthele
aneme atyerremele iperte arlweke-arleke.

Anteater

*You get anteaters in amongst boulders, in
hollows in trees, or in burrows in cracks in
the ground. They've got spines all over
their backs so you have to hit them on the
chest to kill them. You gut one from the
middle of the stomach, pulling out the
milk guts and then closing it up with a
wooden skewer.*

*Then you make a sort of hollow in the
coals and put it on top with its back
facing up, and while it's in the hole you
put coals and ashes on the spines, so
that they will be soft enough to scrape
off. You scrape them off with an axe or
stone scraper like the ones that are used
to make coolamons. When all the spines
have been removed, you cook the
anteater in a round hole in hot earth.*

ARRERNTE: Kere inape
ENGLISH: Anteater
SCIENTIFIC: Tachyglossus aculeatus

46

Kere ankerre

Kere ankerre apele nhenge akwetethe anentye akngerre, atherrkenyenge apeke ahurratyenge apeke. Nhenge renhe apweke-amparre althemele, atne unye atnertenge renhe yanhe inemele arle, apwe altheke-arle atnerteke kwerneme, kele imernte ntheke-iwemele. Lyepe-lyepe arle tyerreke-arle apere walyele apeke imernte renhe imarteye-iwemele itemele. Antere artnwe-iweke-arle nhenge irlweke iperrele, ure apereke-arleke artepe-arrernemele kere tyipe-arle-ileke. Arrwekelenyele irrtyartele atanthewarretyarte, lyete ulkere makitele anteme atyerrewarreme. Atnerte arrwernemele atne-unye tyerreme. Kele atne-unye tyerreke iperrele atnerte apwe althemele atnerte arrwernekele ikwere-arleke ingkerreke anthurre kwernemele kele ntheke-iwemele ure aperrkeke-arleke artnwe-iwetyenhenge. Kele artnwe-iweke iperre tyipe-ilemele atyerremele aperrkeke-arleke artepe arrernemele. Kere yanhe ulkere arunthe anthurrele arlkwentye akngerre, antherremele.

Emu

Emus are around all the time, in green times and dry times. You pluck the feathers out first, then pull out the crop from the stomach, and put in the feathers you've pulled out, and then singe it on the fire. You wrap the milk guts that you've pulled out in something like gum leaves and cook them. When you've got the fat off, you cut the meat up and cook it on fire made from river red gum wood. People before used to spear emus, but nowadays they shoot them with guns. The stomach is opened and the crop pulled out. When this is pulled out the stomach feathers are plucked and put in the stomach. Then the emu is singed on the coals and the fat is removed. When this is done, the meat is cut up and put on the coals to cook. This animal will feed a lot of people, when it's shared out.

NORTH-EASTERN ARRERNTE: Kere ankerre
ENGLISH: Emu
SCIENTIFIC: Dromaius novaehollandiae

Kere artewe

Kere artewe apele uterneke
anentye akngerre, atherrkenye.
Inteltye, angkwerrpme-arlke
akatyerre-arlke arlkwentye
akngerre. Alkereke
irrenhe-irrenhe-arle
akenhe itne.
Ntheke-iwemele,
mpurle
tyerremele,
atne-tye
tyerremele,
atyerreme.

Wild turkey

*There are wild turkeys around in the
summer, and in green times. They
eat grasshoppers, mistletoe berries
and bush currants. They can fly
too. To cook them, you singe the
feathers on the fire, pull out the
crop and the guts from the
backside and then cook them in
hot earth.*

ARRERNTE: Kere artewe
ENGLISH: Wild turkey
SCIENTIFIC: Ardeotis australis

Kere thipe atetherre

Kere atetherre apele akwerrke arlke arle
arlkweme. Atherrkenyele apele arunthe
anthurre anentye akngerre lhere rratyele,
apere urlte akweke-akwekele, apere
urltele, urrenyenke urltele, athenge urltele,
arne urlte arrpenhemele arlke. Akwerrke
aneme alte antethe akweke ware
mperlkere. Renhe ulkere alpmanthele
ware atyerreme ingkerreke anthurre.
Mpenge-irrerlenge atnaltywe tyerremele
arlkweme. Arrpenhele akaperte iwemele
arlkweme, arrpenhemele akenhe
akaperte-inpe arlkweme ikwemeyeke.

ARRERNTE: Kere thipe atetherre
ENGLISH: Budgerigar
SCIENTIFIC: Melopsittacus undulatus

Budgerigar

*Budgerigars are
eaten
when
they are
newly
hatched. In
green times,
there are lots of
them in dry creeks,
in little holes in
gum trees, in gidgees,
ironwoods and other
trees. The newly hatched
birds are covered in white
down. You cook a whole lot of them
in hot earth and when they are cooked
you pull out the guts and eat the bird.
Some people remove the head before
eating the bird but others eat it with the
head because they like the taste.*

48

Kere thipe apelkere

Thipe apelkere ure kwerte-kwerte akenhe re ake arrirlpe akweke. Kere ikwemeye renhe arlkweme. Apwertele weme, arne turele, kwatye arnerreke. Atninetye-akenhe ntheke-iwemele alpmanthele atyerremele arlkweme. Arerre-iperre atyelke akngerre awerne aneme. Kere thipe akweke mape nhenhe-arteke atninetye-akenhe alpmanthele atyerreme. Ampe urreyele tyangayele lyete-ulkere weme.

Crested pigeon

The crested pigeon is a smokey grey colour and has a pointy head. Its meat is very tasty. You get them around waterholes by knocking them down with stones or throwing sticks. You don't gut them, you just singe the feathers off and cook them in hot earth and eat them. There's plenty of meat on the chest. You cook small birds like these in hot earth without gutting them. These days boys shoot them down with shanghais.

ARRERNTE: Kere thipe apelkere
ENGLISH: Crested pigeon
SCIENTIFIC: Ocyphaps lophotes

Kere thipe ilentye

Kere thipe ilentye thipe akngerre re, kere akngerre arlkweme. Kere ampele arlke arlkwenhe-arlkwenhe arelhe akngerrele arlke artengkwelknge-ketye, arrwengkelthe-ketye. Ilentye ikwerele-arlenge kere tyelke akngerre inwengele aneme. Kele alte althemele ntheke-iwemele atyerreme. Iparrpe ware mpenge-irrerlenge atyerremele arlkwerle. Kere yanhe apanpele aneme.

Galah

The galah is a big bird with a lot of meat on it. Kids and women eat it for colds or other sickness. It has a lot of meat on the chest. You pluck the feathers and singe it on a fire, then cook it in hot earth. It cooks very quickly and then you can eat it. This bird lives all over this area.

ARRERNTE: Kere thipe ilentye
ENGLISH: Galah
SCIENTIFIC: Cacatua roseicapilla

Kere thipe awengkere

Kere awengkere nhenge kwatye ipertele anenhe-anenhe. Kere awengkere renhe-arle itne kwatyeke irrpemele itne turele atwetyarte. Lyete ulkere makitele atyerreme. Iparrpe anthurre atyerretyeke re ltare akweke apeke aweme iparrpe anthurre kwatyele irrperle-alhentye akngerre. Kwene ikwerele itne aneme arwerrkentye uyerrerlenge arratintye-alpeme. Renhe atyerreme kere thipe arrpenheme atyerreme arteke, urele. Kere akweke anthurre, kwatye-arteke alyewe-alyewe.

ARRERNTE: Kere thipe awengkere
ENGLISH: Duck (note that 'duck' is often also used by Arrernte people to refer to grebes and other similar birds, the description above is of a grebe)

Duck

Ducks live at waterholes. People used to go into the water and kill the ducks with wooden clubs. These days they shoot them with guns. You have to shoot them really quickly because if they hear even a little noise they dive down into the water. They stay down there and only come out when the noise has stopped. You cook it like you cook other birds, in a fire. It doesn't have much meat on it, and it tastes watery and not very nice.

Kere thipe arlpatye

Kere arlpatye yanhe akenhe arle arlkwenhe-arlkwenhe. Mapele akwele arlkwerrirretyarte, ware apele lyete ulkere. Kere arlpatye akwerrke athenge urlteke inerle, akngerre akenhe arnele anerlenge apwertele weme tyangayele apeke. Kere ilentye-arteke atyerreme alte althemele, urele atyerremele. Iparrpe ware mpenge-irrentye akngerre.

Ring-necked parrot

The ring-necked parrot can also be eaten. People used to eat it a lot but they don't eat it much anymore. You get the baby birds from hollows in ironwood trees or knock down the big ones by throwing rocks at them, maybe with a shanghai. You pluck it and cook it in the fire. It cooks very quickly.

ARRERNTE: Kere thipe arlpatye
ENGLISH: Ring-necked parrot
SCIENTIFIC: Barnardius zonarius

KWATYE
Water

In the arid environment of Central Australia, surival
depends on knowing how to find water. *Kwatye*
includes all forms of water including rain, dew and
running water. It is also used in describing related
things such as frost, ice and steam as well as sources
of water such as rainclouds, rockholes and
soakages in creeks.

Kwatye ngentye

Kwatye uyerrerlenge lherenge, nhenge kwatye ngentye-arle urtnele angernemele iperte-ilemele. Kwatye arrwekele-iperre altyiwemele imernte anemele kwatye re antintyetyeke aneme. Alakenhe-arle kwatye antywenhe-antywenhe.

Soakage water

When the water in the creek dries up, you can still get water by digging down with a coolamon. You scoop out the first lot of water you find (because it's dirty) and then (clean) water flows back into the hole. That's the water you drink.

Kwatye utnarlperte

Kwatye arrpenheme akenhe arne artekerre-ntyele-arle antyweme. Artekerrenge ultakemele antyweme. Kwatye utnarlperte renhe arle akeme. Apmere ikngerre ampinyele alakenhe arunthe.

Water from tree roots

Another kind of water is from the roots of trees. You break the roots open and drink from them. This kind of water is called utnarlperte, and it's common on the eastern side of the Arrernte area.

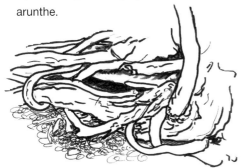

Kwatye wape

Kwatye arrpenhe akenhe antyweme nhenge apere urlteke-arle. Ilepele atwemele apeke apwertele atwemele apeke, apere urlte, awerreke-arleke. Kwatye wape renhe akeme. Kwatyele anhelenge arne arrpe-anenhenge kwatye thelelhetye-akerleme urlte-werne atheke.

Water from tree hollows

You can also drink water from hollows in gum trees. You chop into the solid part of the tree below the opening with a rock or an axe to get it out. This is called wape. *When it rains on the trees, the water runs down into the hollows and stays there.*

53

BUSH FOODS

GLOSSARY

This list includes almost all the words used in Margaret-Mary's descriptions. The meanings given here are fairly basic and do not represent the full range, and readers wanting more information should refer to the *Eastern and Central Arrernte to English Dictionary* (available from IAD Press).

When using this glossary, readers should be aware that most Arrernte words can be used with various endings and that we have not listed all the possible combinations of words and endings here. This means that readers will have to work out for themselves what bits are the basic words and what bits are the endings. The endings are shown here with '-' or '+', as in the ending *-kenhe* 'belonging to'. Verb endings can be quite complicated but there is fairly detailed information on these in the dictionary.

ahe-akngerre	aggressive, dangerous, poisonous
ahekwene	grub from the roots of river red gums
ahelhe	earth, sand, ground, area, region, country
ahentye	1. throat, tube
	2. wanting (something)
ahernenge	grub from the roots of river red gums
aherre	red kangaroo *(Macropus rufus)*
ahurratye	drought, dry time
akakweme	bite, chew on
akantye	end, tip
akaperle	dragon lizard (= kelyawe) *(Ctenophorus nuchalis)*
akaperte	1. head
	2. lid part of native bee nest
akartwe	lid on an *ahernenge* grub's tube
akatyerre	bush raisin, bush sultana *(Solanum centrale)*
ake	head (= akaperte)
akeme	1. cut (something
	2. pick (fruit, etc. from plant)
akenhe, -akenhe	but, 'on the other hand'
akernte	firm, set
akernte-irreme	to get firm, to set
akerte, -akerte	with (something), having (it)
akertne	up high, on top
akethe	outside, clearing, exposed
akethelhe-ileme	make something clear, expose something
aketye-akerleme	cut down something
akikarre	gum found on witchetty bushes
akirtnaneme	pick things off one after another

akngakeme	separate things, sort them out, pick out
aknganeme	be created in the Dreaming
akngerre	big, solid, large
akngerre-apenhe	big one
akngwelye	dog
akweke	small, little; a little bit
akwele	supposedly, 'they reckon…'
akwerneme	put something in
akwerrke	young, new
akwetethe	always
alakenhe	like this, like that, 'this is how…'
alangkwe	bush banana (Marsdenia australis)
alenye	tongue
aletye	raw
alhe	nose
alhe-ilperre	'flat nose' (= arntetherrke)
alhelpe	mallee tree
alheneme	shine or glow on something
alhwenge	burrow
alhwerrpe	winter, cold weather
alkerampwe	gum on mulga trees
alkere	sky, clear sky
alknge	eye
alkngenthe	flame
alparre	1. long and flat
	2. a long, flat wooden dish
alpmanthe	hot earth and ashes beneath a fire used to cook in
alte	hair, fur
altheme	pluck things off, especially feathers
altyartwe	a gap or crack between rocks
altyeye	the edible leaves and stems of a bush banana plant (Marsdenia australis)
altyiweme	tip (liquid) out
altywere	open, opening
alyewe-alyewe	watery tasting, not very nice tasting
amare	mistletoe
amenge	1. fly
	2. native bee
ampe	child
ampeme	burn, cook
ampinye	side, area
amwelye	bearded dragon (lizard) (Pogona vitticeps)
amwerterrpe	young bush bananas
ananerle-alpeme	(things) sitting all in a row

anatye	bush potato *(Ipomea costata)*
ane	and (from English)
aneme	sit, live, be
aneme, -aneme	now, then
anenye	hip part of kangaroo
angerneme	dig, scratch
angkwerrpme	a type of mistletoe
angkweye	old
angkwerrpme	a type of mistletoe
angure	the edible grub inside a bloodwood gall *(Cysticoccus pomiformis)*
anheme	to rain, wet something
anirtneme	(things) sitting in a row
ankere	wax
ankerre	1. emu (= arleye) *(Dromaius novaehollandiae)* 2. coolibah tree. *(Eucalyptus microtheca)*
ankorrutno	edible grub found in the ankerre tree
ankerte	bearded dragon (lizard) *(Pogona vitticeps)*
annge	seed, fruit
anpeme	touch, feel around for (something), reach
ante, -ante	only
ante, ane	and (from English)
antekerre-antekerre	south, southern area
anteme	now, then
antenhe	possum *(Trichosurus vulpecula)*
antere	fat
antethe	flower
anteye, -anteye	still, too, again, exactly
anthelke	dead leaves, bark and sticks
antheme	give
antherreme	share out (lit. give to each other)
anthurre	very, really; real
anthwerrke	guts
antime	still, too, again, exactly
antintyeme	(water) flow in
antyerrke	dried out
antyerrke-irreme	to dry out
antyweme	drink
antywenhe-antywenhe	things to do with drinking; drink, drinker, etc.
anwerne	we (more than two people)
anyente	one, alone
anyente(lhe)-ileme	bring things together into one; join, put together
anyente-ame-anyente	one by one; few and far between
apanpe	all over the place, everywhere

apeke	maybe, probably, must, might
apele	Indicates that speakers know themselves that what they are saying is true, and are not just saying what they have heard from others
apelkere	crested pigeon *(Ocyphaps lophotes)*
apenteme	follow
aperaltye	waxy white food on river red gum leaves
aperarnte	honeydew from red gum
apere	river red gum *(Eucalyptus camaldulensis)*
aperlape	conkerberry
apernelhenhelhenhe	something which is rubbed or smeared on
aperneme	rub or smear something on
aperrke	hot coals, charcoal
aperrkinpe-aperrkinpe	(food) mixed up with bits of the coals they were cooked in
apmere	place, country, region
apmwe	a general word for snakes
apurte	a clump, ball; together
apurte-ileme	make something into a clump or ball
apwe	emu feathers
apwernkeme	split open
apwerte	rock, hill; money
apwerte-apwerte	a rocky or hilly area
arelhe	woman
areme	see, look at, watch
arenge	euro *(Macroups robustus)*
arenye, -arenye	from, belonging to, associated with
arerre	chest
areye, -areye	many, few
arlarte	thick, bushy (tree)
arlatyeye	pencil yam *(Vigna lanceolata)*
arle	1. holes in the ground above a honeyant nest 2. plant
arle, -arle	that (as in 'the one that...' or 'said that...')
arleke, -arleke	onto (something)
arlenge	distant, a long way
arlepayte	edible grub found on the prickly wattle
arlepe	prickly wattle *(Acacia victoriae)*
arletye	raw, uncooked; not ripe
arlewatyerre	goanna *(Varanus gouldii)*
arlke, -arlke	too, and, also.
arlketyerre	dead finish tree *(Acacia tetragonophylla)*
arlkweme	eat; chew
arlpatye	ring-necked parrot, Port Lincoln parrot *(Banardius zonarius)*

arlpe	= alpmanthe
arlpelhe	wing; feather; leaf
arlpentye	long, tall
arlpere-aneme	hang on something
arlperrampwe	gum from the whitewood tree
arlperrayte	edible grub found on the whitewood tree
arlperre	whitewood tree *(Atalaya hemiglauca)*
arlware	inflated; swollen up
arlwe	roundish rock; round
arlwileme	make into a roundish lump; gather together into a pile
arne	tree, wood, thing
arnerre	rockhole with water in it
arnkarre	steep banks of a creek
arnkwerrknge	cracks in the ground
arntape	thick bark
arntarlkwe	fork in tree, branches
arnteme	ache
arnterre	colony wattle *(Acacia murrayana)*
arntetherrke	carpet snake
arnweketye	conkerberry *(Carissa lanceolata)*
arrakerte	mouth
arralkeme	open your mouth; yawn
arrankweye	bush plum *(Santalum lanceolatum)*
arrateme	come out, go out
arreme	native bee larva, louse
arrerlkere	light-coloured, clear
arrerneme	put (something) down, put (it) in
arrernirtnaneme	put (things) down one after another
arrinkeme	give you an appetite
arrirlpe	sharp
arrirtne	name
arriwe	entrance, opening
arrkerneme	taste (something), try (it)
arrkernke	desert oak tree *(Allocasuarina decaisneana)*
arrkirlpangkwerle	insect gall on bloodwood tree; bush coconut
arrpe-anenhe	each, every one
arrpeme	trim something with a blade
arrpenhe	other, different, some
arrpenheme	other, different
arrurelheme	(things) drop onto the ground
arrutnenge	wild passionfruit *(Capparis spinosa var. nummularia)*
arrwe	rock wallaby *(Petrogale lateralis)*
arrwekele	in front, first, before
arrwekele-iperre	something in front or from before

arrwekelenye	the first one, the one in front; ancestors
arrwengkelthe	poison, illness
arrwerneme	gut an emu
arteke, -arteke	like something, similar to it
artekerre	root of a plant or tree
arteme	cover or bury something, build something
artengkwelknge	head cold, snot
artepe	back
artetye	mulga tree *(Acacia aneura)*
artetye-artetye	area with a lot of mulga trees
artewe	bush turkey, bustard *(Ardeotis australis)*
artitye	teeth
artnwe	emu fat
artnwe-iweme	remove emu fat
arunthe	many, a lot of (things)
arwakeme	lever (something) up
arwengalkere	honey from wild bees; sugarbag
arwerrkentye	noise
ataltyakwerle	insect gall on mulga trees; mulga apple
atantheme	poke, pierce
ateme	burst out, burst forward
atetherre	budgerigar *(Melopsittacus undulatus)*
atheke, -atheke	in the direction of, towards
atheme	grind
atheneme	lay something down
athengayte	grub in ironwood tree
athenge	ironwood tree *(Acacia estrophiolata)*
athenge arlperle	gum found on ironwood tree
atherrame	two, both
atherre	two
atherrke	green grass
atherrke-atherrke	green, yellow
atherrkenye	green time, after rain
athetheke	red
athetheke-athetheke	reddish; pink, orange
athirnte	flat rock
athnwerte-ileme	curl something up
atnakerte	backside
atnaltye	part of the guts
atnartenge	base of (e.g. tree)
atne	droppings, shit
atne-ineme, atnineme	gut an animal
atne-ite	the guts pulled out through the mouth
atne-tye	the guts pulled out through the backside

atne-unye	crop (bird's guts)
atneltyeme	squeeze the guts out of caterpillars
atnerte	stomach, belly
atnetye	edible root of bush banana plant
atnilhe	bum
atningke	many, a lot of (things)
atniweme	1. gut an animal
	2. call something, refer to it as
atnulke	part of the guts
atnware	heel
atnyematye	edible grub from witchetty bush
atnyeme	1. witchetty bush
	2. fall, drop down
atnyentye	moon, moonlight
atnyerampwe	gum on *atnyere* tree
atnyere	supplejack tree *(Ventilago viminalis)*
atwakeye	bush orange *(Capparis mitchellii)*
atweme	hit; kill
atwetye	1. kangaroo joey
	2. see *+ke-atwetye*
atyankerne	type of mistletoe
atyerreme	1. cook
	2. shoot
atyete	soft
atyunpe	perentie *(Varanus giganteus)*
awantyeme	lick
awatentye-awatentye	waxy-looking
awele-awele	bush tomato
awelheme	feel
aweme	listen, hear; understand
awengkere	duck, grebe, and some similar birds
awerne	one (as in 'big one')
awerre	solid part of something
awerrpe	juices from a kangaroo after it is cooked
awethe	again, more
ayelpayerneme	twist or wind something up
ayenpe	skin
ayepe	tar vine. *(Boerhavia spp.)*
ayepe-arenye	caterpillar found on the ayepe plant
ayerrere	north
ikelhe	firm, thick, solid; lump, blob of something
ikerrke-iwelheme	stick onto something
ikiweme	scrape crust or crusty stuff off something
ikngerre	east

ikwemeye	sweet, tasty
ikwere	for him/her/it; onto it
ikwere-arleke	onto it
ikwere-werle	to it, towards it
ikwerenge	from him/her/it; there; then
ikwerenhe	his/her(s)/its
ileme	1. say, tell someone something
	2. make something be a certain way
ilentye	galah
ilepe	stone axe
ilkwarte	bush cucumber
iltye	hand
iltyingke	a bundle of things held in the hand
ilweme	die
imarteye-iweme	wrap something up
imernte, imerte	then
impeme	leave alone, leave behind
inape	anteater
ineme	get, take
ingke	foot; footprints
ingkerreke, ingkirreke	all, every
ingkwelye	shrivelled up, wrinkled
ingwenenge	edible grub from trunk and branches of river red gums
-inpe	with, including
inte	wooden stick used as a probe, skewer, or spindle
intelhentye	pattern, design, colour
inteltye	grasshopper
inteme	lie down
interlpe	wooden skewer
intyerrke	dry, dried out
inurle	spider
inwenge	chest
iparrpe	quickly
iperneme	sool a dog onto something, use a dog to hunt
iperre, -iperre	after, because of
iperte	1. hole
	2. steep, deep
iperte-ileme	make a hole
irlweke	native pine tree
irlweme	take something down off something
irrarle	cocoon
irreme	become (some way), be (that way)
irrkngelhe	bark
irrpeme	enter, put part of yourself in something

irrtnye	skin, peel
irrtnye-iweme	skin or peel something
irrtyarte	spear
iteme	cook; light a fire
itepe-itere	side of something
itere	side of something
itne	they (more than two, subject)
itnenhe	they (more than two, object of le type verb)
iwomo	throw something away
kalikewe	cloth (from English 'calico')
kanyengarre	scraper, adze, chisel
+ke	1. for (something)
	2. (do something) at or to (something)
	3. into, onto
	4. (on a verb) already happened, in the past
+ke-amparre	first
+ke-arleke	onto
+ke-atwetye	up until
kele	finished; already; then
kelyawe	dragon lizard
-kenhe	belonging to
kenhe, akenhe, -akenhe	but, 'on the other hand'
kere	meat, game animal
-ketye	to avoid (something)
kutyeme	collect, pick things up
kwarte	egg
kwatye	water
kwatyelhe-ileme	sprinkle water on something
kwekareme	suck
kwene	inside, under
kwenhe	definitely, clearly
kwenye	not
kwerneme	swallow
kwerte-kwerte	smokey grey
+le	1. Indicates the one doing the action of a transitive verb
	2. at, in, on
+le-arlenge	1. with, accompanied by
	2. in (a container)
+le-mpele	through (something)
lernelhe-ileme	shake something to get things off it
lerneme	shake things off something, scatter them
lhere	creek, river
ltare	sharp noise; click, tap, knock
lterre	shin

lterrke	tight, strong, hard
ltyentye	beefwood tree
lyapeme	grow, sprout
lyarnte-ileme	make something round
lyarrtye	dried out
lyeke	prickle, thorn, quill
lyeke-lyeke	prickly; rough
lyepe-lyepe	small intestines
lyerle	gravelly sand
lyete	now, today, these days
lyete-ulkere	these days, more recently
makite	gun, rifle (probably from English 'musket')
mape	a number of things, group (from English 'mob')
marle	girl, female
+me	(on verbs) happening now, happens
merne	food from plants, fruit, vegetables
mpenge	cooked, ripe
mpepe	middle
mperlkere	white
mperlkere-mperlkere	whitish
mpurle	part of bird's guts, crop
mpwareme	make, do, fix
mwanyeme	a type of bush tomato plant
mwelpemwerneye	sticky
mwerrantye	well, properly
mwerre	good,
name	grass
+nge	1. from
	2. than
	3. at, on, in
ngentye	soakage, a hole dug in a creekbed to get water
ngkwarle	sweet honey-like food
nhenge	'that (one)', 'you know (the one)'
nhenhe	here; this one
ntange	edible seeds
nterlpenternentye	spotted
nterneme	pierce or spear something
ntewale	nectar from bloodwood flowers
nteweme	dash or flick something against tree, ground, etc.
ntheke-iweme	toss something on flames to singe or sear it
nthirrpmarre-iwelheme	stick to something
ntyarlke	a type of caterpillar, elephant grub
-ntyele	from
ntyeme	smell, give off a smell

ntyere	flat area near a creek that flood waters run over into
ntyerneme	smell something.
payenteme-ileme	find something (from English)
pmerlpe	quandong
pmware	a type of wooden scoop for digging
pmwelkere	blue-grey colour
pwenge-irreme	close your eyes
pweralheme	a type of mistletoe
rapite	rabbit (from English)
rarle	= re + arle
re	he/she/it (doer of the action)
renhe	him/her/it (the one the action is done to)
+rle	(on verbs) would happen, typically happens
rlkerte	sick
rlpmerre	drop, drip (of liquid)
rratye	dry (creek)
teke-aneme	be spread out to dry
teke-iweme	put something out to dry
terte	damp earth, sand
thankweme	scoop water etc. out
thelelheme	drip, run
thelelhetye-akerleme	drip or run down
thipe	fleshy flying creatures; birds (not emus), bats
tile	tail (from English)
tiweme	singe the fur off a kangaroo on a fire
tneme	stand
tnetye-akerleme	(shaft) run down (lit. stand down)
tnyeme	dig
tnyileme	kill something
tunpere	a type of grass that you can get a small hook from to get gum tree grubs out
ture	wooden throwing stick
turre	higher ground, especially next to creeks
tyampite	tin can
tyangaye	slingshot, shanghai
tyape	edible grub
tyarre-ineme	drag or pull something out
tyarrpe	crack, slit
+tyarte	(on verbs) used to happen, used to do this
+tyeke	(on verbs) to do this, so that this happens
tyelke	flesh, muscle
+tyenhe	(on verbs) will happen, will do this
tyerraye	cicada
tyerreme	pull something out

tyerrtye	body, person, Aboriginal person
tyipe-ileme	make something into pieces
ulkantyerrknge	edible flowers of the wild banana vine
ulkere, -ulkere	-ish, that sort of thing, -er (as in 'bigger')
ulkerte	perentie
ulpe-ileme	make something into a fine or smooth texture
ulpere	a hollow, hole; especially in a tree
ulperre	(lying) on stomach
ultakeme	break, break off
ulte	side of body, ribs
ulyawe	a type of pigweed
ulyentye	shade
ulyepere	thigh
unekele	staying out overnight
untarne-untarne	yellow
unte	you (one person)
untheme	walk around, wander around; look for something
untye	back of the neck
untyeyampe	corkwood tree nectar
untyeye	corkwood tree (Hakea eyreana, H. suberea)
unye	crop (bird's guts)
ure	fire, things related to fire
urewe	running water, floodwaters
urltampe	native bee honey
urlte	hole or hollow in a tree
urrenyenke	gidgee tree
urreye	boy, male animal
urrkale	mulga country
-urrke	first
urrknge	mushy stuff
urrknge-ileme	mash something up
urrpere	crack in the ground, etc.
urrperle	dark colour, black
urrperle-irreme	turn a dark colour
urrperle-urrperle	darkish colour
urrpetye	three, a few
urrpme	ripples, parallel lines
urteke	short
urtethe	lower back
urtne	wooden carrying dish
urure-weme	rub between your hands
uterne	sun, summer, hot weather
uthene	and (joins two things only)
utnarlperte	water found in the roots of certain trees

utnerrengatye	edible grub found in the *utnerrenge* bush
utnerrenge	emu bush
utnheme	collect (fruit, etc.), bite (something)
utyene	sore, injury, rash
utyerrke	wild fig *(Ficus platypoda)*
utyewe	thin, skinny
uyerreme	disappear, die, run out
wale	well (from English)
walye	green branches, leaves, etc.
waneye	only, except that…
wape	water found in hollows in trees
ware	only, no reason
weme	hit something with something you throw at it
werlatye	breast, milk
-werle	to, towards
-werne	to, towards
yalke	wild onion *(Cyperus bulbosa)*
yanhe	that, there (not too far away)
yerrampe	honeyant *(Melophorus camponotus)*
yerre	ant

PRONUNCIATION OF FOOD NAMES

It is not really possible to give an accurate representation of the pronunciation just using English 'phonetics', so the following should only be taken as a very rough guide.

For the purposes of this guide only:

➢ Stressed (stronger) syllables are in uppercase, e.g. JEE. Don't put too much emphasis on the other parts of a word.
➢ 'uh' is something like the 'e' in 'magnet' or sometimes the 'u' in 'but'.
➢ 'ah' is like 'a' in 'father'.
➢ 'oo' is like in 'cook'.
➢ 'ai' is like in 'train'.
➢ 'er' is like in an American pronunciation of 'Bert'.
➢ 'or' is like in 'port'.
➢ 'rr' is a hard or rolled 'r' like in Scottish English.
➢ 'r' is like the ordinary Australian English 'r' as in 'bearing'.
➢ The sound written 'h' in Arrernte is not in English and is impossible to get close to it in English 'phonetics'. It is actually more like modern French 'r'. English 'h' will have to do here, but it is quite different.

ahekwene	uh-HUH-koon-uh ('oo' as in 'cook')
ahernenge	uh-HER-nuhng-uh ('ng' as in 'hung' not 'hunger')
aherre	uh-HUH-rruh
akatyerre	uh-KAH-juh-rruh
akikarre	uh-KEE-kah-rruh
alangkwe	uh-LAHNG-gwuh
alhelpe-arenye	uh-LUHLL-pah-rin-yuh (1st 'L' touching top teeth)
alkerampwe	uhl-KUH-rahm-bwuh
altyeye	uhl-JEE-uh
amwelye	uh-MOOL-yuh ('OO' as in 'wool')
anatye	uhn-NAH-juh
angkwerrpme	uhng-GORRP-muh
ankerre	uhn-GUH-rruh
ankerrutne	uhn-GUH-rrort-nuh
ankerte	uhn-GER-tuh
antenhe	uhn-DUH-nuh (last 'n' touching top teeth)
apelkere	uh-PUHL-kuh-ruh
aperaltye	uh-PUH-rahl-juh
aperarnte	uh-PUH-rarn-duh
aperlape	uh-PER-lah-puh
arenge	uh-RUHNG-uh ('ng' as in 'hung' not 'hunger')
arlatyeye	ar-LAH-jee/ ai-LAH-jee

arlepayte	ar-LUH-pay-tuh/ ai-LUH-pay-tuh
arlepe	ar-LUH-puh/ ai-LUH-puh
arlewatyerre	ar-LOW-ah-juh-rruh/ ai-LOW-ah-juh-rruh ('OW' like in 'slow')
arlketyerre	arl-KUH-juh-rruh/ ail-KUH-juh-rruh
arlpatye	arl-PAH-juh/ ail-PAH-juh
arlperle	arl-PER-luh/ ail-PER-luh
arlperrampwe	arl-PUH-rrahm-bwuh/ ail-PUH-rrahm-bwuh
arlperrayte	arl-PUH-rruh/ ail-PUH-rruh
arntetherrke	arn-DUH-tuhrr-kuh/ ain-DUH-tuhrr-kuh ('t' touching top teeth)
arnweketye	ar-NOOK-uh-juh/ ai-NOOK-uh-juh ('oo' as in 'book')
arrankweye	uh-RRAHN-gwee
arrkirlpangkwerle	arr-KEEL-pahng-goorl-uh
arrutnenge	uh-RRORT-nuhng-uh ('ng' as in 'hung' not 'hunger')
arrwe	ahrr-wuh
artetye	ar-TIJ-uh/ ai-TIJ-uh
artewe	ar-TOW-uh/ ai-TOW-uh ('OW' as in 'slow')
arwengalkere	uh-ROONG-ahl-kuh-ruh
ataltyakwerle	uh-TAHL-jah-koorl-uh
atetherre	uh-TUH-tuh-rruh (2nd 't' touching top teeth)
athengayte	uh-TUHNG-ai-tuh (1st 'T' touching top teeth)
athenge	uh-TUHNG-uh ('T' touching top teeth)
atnetye	uht-NUH-juh
atnyematye	uht-NYUH-mah-juh
atnyerampwe	uht-NYUH-rahm-bwuh
atwakeye	uh-TWAH-gee ('g' as in 'go')
atyankerne	uh-CHARN-ger-nuh
atyunpe	uh-CHORN-puh
awele-awele	uh-WOOL-uh-WOOL-uh
awengkere	uh-WOONG-guh-ruh ('oo' as in 'wool'; 'ng' as in 'hung' not 'hunger')
ayepe	uh-YIP-uh
ayepe-arenye	uh-YIP-uh-rin-yuh
ilentye	il-LUHN-juh
ilkwarte	il-KWAR-tuh
inape	in-NAH-puh
ingwenenge	ing-WOON-uhng-uh ('oo' as in 'wool')
kaperle	KAH-per-luh
kelyawe	KUHL-yow ('ow' as in 'how')
kere	KUH-ruh
kwatye	KWAH-juh
merne	MER-nuh
mwanyeme	MWAHN-yuh-muh

ngentye	NGUHN-juh ('NG' as in 'sing')
ngkwarle	ng-GWAR-luh ('ng' as in 'sing')
ntange	nn-DAHNG-uh ('ng' as in 'hung' not 'hunger')
ntewale	nn-DOW-ah-luh ('OW' as in 'slow')
ntyarlke	nn-JARL-kuh
pmerlpe	PMERL-puh (not puh-MERL-puh)
pweralheme	POOR-ah-luh-muh ('oo' as in 'book'; 'l' touching top teeth)
thipe	TEP-uh ('T' touching top teeth; 'E' as in 'bed')
tyape	CHAH-puh
tyerraye	CHUH-rrai
ulkantyerrknge	ool-KAHN-jerrk-nguh ('oo' as in 'wool'; 'ng' as in 'hung' not 'hunger')
ulkerte	ool-KER-tuh ('oo' as in 'wool')
ulyawe	ool-YOW-uh ('OW' as in 'how')
untyeyampe	oon-JEE-ahm-buh ('oo' as in 'book')
urltampe	oorl-DAHM-buh ('oo' as in 'wool')
utnarlperte	oot-NARL-ber-tuh ('oo' as in 'book')
utnerrengatye	oot-NUH-rruhng-ah-juh ('oo' as in 'book')
utyerrke	oo-CHERR-kuh ('oo' as in 'book')
wape	WAH-puh
yalke	YAHL-kuh
yerrampe	YUH-rrahm buh